Learn
JavaScript®
and AJAX
with w3schools

Hege Refsnes, Ståle Refsnes, Kai Jim Refsnes,
and Jan Egil Refsnes
with Kelly Dobbs Henthorne

WILEY
Wiley Publishing, Inc.

Learn JavaScript® and AJAX with w3schools

Published by
Wiley Publishing, Inc.
111 River Street
Hoboken, NJ 07030-5774
www.wiley.com

Copyright © 2010 by Wiley Publishing, Inc., Indianapolis, Indiana

Published simultaneously in Canada

ISBN: 978-0-470-61194-4

LOC/CIP: 2010925161

Manufactured in the United States of America

10 9 8 7 6 5 4 3 2 1

For general information on our other products and services please contact our Customer Care Department within the United States at (877) 762-2974, outside the United States at (317) 572-3993 or fax (317) 572-4002.

Wiley also publishes its books in a variety of electronic formats. Some content that appears in print may not be available in electronic books.

Library of Congress CIP Data is available from the publisher.

w3schools Authors/Editors

w3schools' mission is to publish well-organized and easy-to-understand online tutorials based on the W3C Web standards.

Hege Refsnes

Hege is a writer and editor for w3schools. She works to improve the usability and accessibility of the Web.

Hege has been writing tutorials for w3schools since 1998.

Ståle Refsnes

Ståle has ten years of Internet development experience, developing all the Web-based solutions for The Norwegian Handball Federation.

Ståle has been writing tutorials for w3schools since 1999.

Kai Jim Refsnes

Kai Jim has been around computers since childhood, working with them since the age of 14.

He has been writing tutorials for w3schools since completing a bachelor's degree in information technology in 2005.

Jan Egil Refsnes

Jan Egil is the president and founder of w3schools.

He is a senior system developer with a master's degree in information technology and more than 30 years of computing experience.

"Jani" has supervised a large number of company-critical development projects for oil companies like Amoco, British Petroleum, ELF, Halliburton, and Brown & Root. He has also developed computer-based solutions for more than 20 governmental institutions like The National Library, Norwegian High Schools, The State Hospital, and many others.

Jani started w3schools in 1998.

Credits

Acquisitions Editor
Scott Meyers

Production
Abshier House

Technical Editor
Harry Buss

Copy Editor
Abshier House

Associate Director of Marketing
David Mayhew

Production Manager
Tim Tate

Vice President and Executive Group Publisher
Richard Swadley

Vice President and Executive Publisher
Barry Pruett

Associate Publisher
Jim Minatel

Project Coordinator, Cover
Lynsey Stanford

Proofreading and Indexing
Abshier House

Cover Designer
Michael Trent

TABLE OF CONTENTS

INTRODUCTION

Welcome to *Learn JavaScript and Ajax with w3schools*. This book is for Web site designers and builders who want to learn to add interactivity to their Web pages with JavaScript and Ajax.

w3schools (www.w3schools.com), is one of the top Web destinations to learn JavaScript and many other key Web languages. Founded in 1998, w3schools' tutorials are recommended reading in more than 100 universities and high schools all over the world. This book is a great companion to the JavaScript and Ajax tutorials on the w3schools site, which were written by Jan Egil Refsnes, Ståle Refsnes, Kai Jim Refsnes, and Hege Refsnes.

Like the w3schools online tutorials, this book features a brief presentation of each topic, trading lengthy explanations for abundant examples showcasing each key feature. This book, as well as other w3schools books published by Wiley, features straight-forward and concise tutorials on each topic from which the beginning Web developer can easily learn. All of the book's content is derived from w3schools' accurate, user-tested content used by millions of learners every month.

JavaScript

JavaScript is *the* scripting language of the Web. JavaScript is used in millions of Web pages to add functionality, validate forms, detect browsers, and much more. JavaScript is the most popular scripting language on the Internet and works in all major browsers, such as Internet Explorer, Firefox, Chrome, Opera, and Safari.

What You Should Already Know

Before you continue you should have a basic understanding of HTML.

If you want to study this subject first, please read *Learn HTML and CSS with w3schools*.

What Is JavaScript?

- ▸▸ JavaScript was designed to add interactivity to HTML pages.
- ▸▸ JavaScript is a scripting language.
- ▸▸ A scripting language is a lightweight programming language.
- ▸▸ JavaScript is usually embedded directly into HTML pages.

- JavaScript is an interpreted language (means that scripts execute without preliminary compilation).
- Everyone can use JavaScript without purchasing a license.

Are Java and JavaScript the Same?

No, they are not. Java and JavaScript are two completely different languages in both concept and design.

Java (developed by Sun Microsystems) is a powerful and much more complex programming language in the same category as C and C++.

What Can JavaScript Do?

- **JavaScript gives HTML designers a programming tool.** HTML authors are normally not programmers, but JavaScript is a scripting language with a very simple syntax. Almost anyone can put small "snippets" of code into their HTML pages.
- **JavaScript can put dynamic text into an HTML page.** A JavaScript statement like document.write("<h1>" + name + "</h1>") can write a variable text into an HTML page.
- **JavaScript can react to events.** A JavaScript script can be set to execute when something happens, like when a page has finished loading or when a user clicks on an HTML element.
- **JavaScript can read and write HTML elements.** A JavaScript script can read and change the content of an HTML element.
- **JavaScript can be used to validate data.** A JavaScript script can be used to validate form data before it is submitted to a server. This saves the server from extra processing.
- **JavaScript can be used to detect the visitor's browser.** A JavaScript script can be used to detect the visitor's browser, and depending on the browser, load another page specifically designed for that browser.
- **JavaScript can be used to create cookies.** A JavaScript script can be used to store and retrieve information on the visitor's computer.

The Real Name Is ECMAScript

JavaScript's official name is ECMAScript, which is developed and maintained by the ECMA International organization.

The language was invented by Brendan Eich at Netscape (with Navigator 2.0) and has appeared in all Netscape and Microsoft browsers since 1996.

2

ECMA-262 is the official JavaScript standard. The development of ECMA-262 started in 1996, and the first edition of was adopted by the ECMA General Assembly in June 1997. The standard was approved as an international ISO (ISO/IEC 16262) standard in 1998.

The development of the standard is still in progress.

AJAX

AJAX equals Asynchronous JavaScript and XML.

AJAX is based on JavaScript and HTTP requests. AJAX is not a new programming language, but a new way to use existing standards.

AJAX is the art of trading data with a Web server, and changing parts of a Web page, without reloading the whole page.

What You Should Already Know

Before you continue you should have a basic understanding of the following:

▸▸ HTML

▸▸ JavaScript

If you want to study these subjects first, find the tutorials on the w3schools home page.

AJAX = Asynchronous JavaScript and XML

AJAX is not a new programming language, but a new technique for creating better, faster, and more interactive Web applications.

With AJAX, a JavaScript can communicate directly with the server, with the XMLHttpRequest object. With this object, a JavaScript can trade data with a Web server, without reloading the page.

AJAX uses asynchronous data transfer (HTTP requests) between the browser and the Web server, allowing Web pages to request small bits of information from the server instead of whole pages.

The AJAX technique makes Internet applications smaller, faster, and more user friendly.

AJAX Is Based on Internet Standards

AJAX is based on the following Web standards:

▸▸ JavaScript

▸▸ XML

▶ HTML

▶ CSS

AJAX applications are browser- and platform-independent.

AJAX Is About Better Internet-Applications

Internet applications have many benefits over desktop applications: They can reach a larger audience; they are easier to install and support; and they are easier to develop.

However, Internet applications are not always as "rich" and user friendly as traditional desktop applications.

With AJAX, Internet applications can be made richer and more user friendly.

Start Using AJAX Today

There is nothing new to learn. AJAX is based on existing standards. These standards have been used by developers for several years.

How To Use This Book

Throughout this book, you will see several icons:

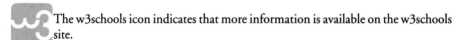

The Try It Yourself icon indicates an opportunity for you to practice what you've just learned. The code and examples under this icon come from examples on the w3schools site, which allow you to make changes to the code and see the results immediately. You do not have to type in the code examples in this book; you will find them all on the w3schools site.

The w3schools icon indicates that more information is available on the w3schools site.

This icon indicates where you will find further information about a topic that is covered more thoroughly elsewhere within the book.

This book is divided into five sections:

▶ Section I: JavaScript Basic

▶ Section II: JavaScript Objects

▶ Section III: JavaScript Advanced

▶ Section IV: AJAX Basic

▶ Section V: SectionAJAX Advanced

If you're anxious to improve your Web pages and to add some interactivity, jump right in with JavaScript Basic. Plenty of examples and opportunities to try things await, and w3schools will be right there when you need them!

Section I
JavaScript
Basic

CHAPTER 1

JAVASCRIPT HOW TO AND WHERE TO

In This Chapter

❑ How To Put a JavaScript into an HTML Page

❑ How To Handle Simple Browsers

❑ Where To Put the JavaScript

❑ Using an External JavaScript

The HTML `<script>` tag is used to insert a JavaScript into an HTML page.

How To Put a JavaScript into an HTML Page

The following example shows how to use JavaScript to write text on a Web page.

The result of this script is shown in Figure 1.1.

```
<html>
<body>
<script type="text/javascript">
document.write("Hello World!");
</script>
</body>
</html>
```

```
Hello World!
```

Figure 1.1

Here's your first opportunity to personalize JavaScript. Change the "Hello World" text to "Happy, Happy, Joy, Joy!" and see what happens. The result of your changes is shown in Figure 1.2.

```
<html>
<body>
<script type="text/javascript">
document.write("Happy, Happy, Joy, Joy!");
</script>
</body>
</html>
```

```
Happy, Happy, Joy, Joy!
```

Figure 1.2

The following example shows how to add HTML tags to the JavaScript. The result of this code is shown in Figure 1.3.

```
<html>
<body>
<script type="text/javascript">
document.write("<h1>Hello World!</h1>");
</script>
</body>
</html>
```

Hello World!

Figure 1.3

Continuing with our happier version of the code, change the "Hello World!" text to "Happy, Happy, Joy, Joy!" and see what happens. The result of your changes is shown in Figure 1.4.

Try it yourself >>

```
<html>
<body>
<script type="text/javascript">
document.write("<h1>Happy, Happy, Joy, Joy!</h1>");
</script>
</body>
</html>
```

Happy, Happy, Joy, Joy!

Figure 1.4

To insert a JavaScript into an HTML page, we use the `<script>` tag. Inside the `<script>` tag we use the type attribute to define the scripting language.

So, `<script type="text/javascript">` and `</script>` tell where the Java-Script starts and ends:

```
<html>
<body>
<script type="text/javascript">
...
</script>
</body>
</html>
```

The `document.write` command is a standard JavaScript command for writing output to a page.

When you type the `document.write` command between the `<script>` and `</script>` tags, the browser will recognize it as a JavaScript command and execute the code line. In this case, the browser writes Hello World! to the page:

```
<html>
<body>
<script type="text/javascript">
document.write("Hello World!");
```

(continued)

11

(continued)

```
    </script>
    </body>
    </html>
```

> **N O T E** If we had not typed the `<script>` tag, the browser would have treated
> the `document.write("Hello World!")` command as pure text and would just
> write the entire line on the page, as shown in Figure 1.5.

```
document.write("Hello World!");
```

Figure 1.5

How to Handle Simple Browsers

Browsers that do not support JavaScript will display JavaScript as page content.

To prevent them from doing this and as a part of the JavaScript standard, the HTML comment tag should be used to "hide" the JavaScript.

Just add an HTML comment tag `<!--` before the first JavaScript statement, and an end-of–comment tag `-->` after the last JavaScript statement, like this:

```
<html>
<body>
<script type="text/javascript">
<!--
document.write("Hello World!");
//-->
</script>
</body>
</html>
```

The two forward slashes at the end of comment line (`//`) comprise the JavaScript comment symbol. This prevents JavaScript from executing the `-->` tag.

Where to Put the JavaScript

JavaScripts in a page will be executed immediately while the page loads into the browser. This is not always what we want. Sometimes we want to execute a script when a page loads, or at a later event, such as when a user clicks a button. When this is the case we put the script inside a function. You will learn about functions in Chapter 10, "JavaScript Functions."

Scripts in <head>

Scripts to be executed when they are called, or when an event is triggered, are placed in functions.

Put your functions in the head section. This way they are all in one place, and they do not interfere with page content. The resulting alert box is shown in Figure 1.6.

Try it yourself >>

```
<html>
<head>
<script type="text/javascript">
function message()
{
alert("This alert box was called with the onload event");
}
</script>
</head>

<body onload="message()">
</body>
</html>
```

Figure 1.6

Scripts in <body>

If you don't want your script to be placed inside a function, or if your script should write page content, it should be placed in the body section. Figure 1.7 shows the result.

13

```
<html>
<head>
</head>

<body>
<script type="text/javascript">
document.write("This message is written by JavaScript");
</script>
</body>

</html>
```

This message is written by JavaScript

Figure 1.7

Scripts in <head> and <body>

You can place an unlimited number of scripts in your document, so you can have scripts in both the body and the head section.

```
<html>
<head>
<script type="text/javascript">
function message()
{
alert("This alert box was called with the onload event");
}
</script></head>
<body onload="message()">
<script type="text/javascript">
document.write("This message is written by JavaScript");
</script>
</body>

</html>
```

Using an External JavaScript

If you want to run the same JavaScript on several pages without having to write the same script on every page, you can write a JavaScript in an external file.

Save the external JavaScript file with a .js file extension. Your results are shown in Figure 1.8.

> **N O T E** The external script cannot contain the <script> tag!

Try it yourself >>

To use the external script, point to the .js file in the src attribute of the <script> tag as shown:

```
<html>
<head>
<script type="text/javascript" src="xxx.js"></script>
</head>
<body>
</body>
</html>
```

This text was written by an external script!

Figure 1.8

> **N O T E** Remember to place the script exactly where you normally would write the script!

CHAPTER 2

JAVASCRIPT STATEMENTS AND COMMENTS

In This Chapter

❏ JavaScript Code

❏ JavaScript Blocks

❏ JavaScript Multiline Comments

❏ Using Comments To Prevent Execution

❏ Using Comments at the End of a Line

JavaScript is a sequence of statements to be executed by the browser. Unlike HTML, JavaScript is case-sensitive; therefore, watch your capitalization closely when you write JavaScript statements and create or call variables, objects, and functions.

JavaScript Statements

A JavaScript statement is a command to a browser. The purpose of the command is to tell the browser what to do.

The following JavaScript statement tells the browser to write "Hello Dolly" to the Web page:

```
document.write("Hello Dolly");
```

It is normal to add a semicolon at the end of each executable statement. Most people think this is a good programming practice, and most often you will see this in JavaScript examples on the Web.

The semicolon is optional (according to the JavaScript standard), and the browser is supposed to interpret the end of the line as the end of the statement. You often will see examples without the semicolon at the end.

16

> **N O T E** Using semicolons makes it possible to write multiple statements on one line, although good programming practice encourages placing only one statement per line.

JavaScript Code

JavaScript code (or just JavaScript) is a sequence of JavaScript statements. Each statement is executed by the browser in the sequence it is written.

This example will write a heading and two paragraphs to a Web page as shown in Figure 2.1.

Try it yourself >>

```
<html>
<body>

<script type="text/javascript">
document.write("<h1>This is a heading</h1>");
document.write("<p>This is a paragraph.</p>");
document.write("<p>This is another paragraph.</p>");
</script>

</body>
</html>
```

This is a heading

This is a paragraph.

This is another paragraph.

Figure 2.1

JavaScript Blocks

JavaScript statements can be grouped together in blocks. Blocks start with a left curly bracket { and end with a right curly bracket }.

The purpose of a block is to make the sequence of statements execute together.

The following example writes a heading and two paragraphs to a Web page as shown in Figure 2.2.

17

```
<html>
<body>

<script type="text/javascript">
{
document.write("<h1>This is a heading</h1>");
document.write("<p>This is a paragraph.</p>");
document.write("<p>This is another paragraph.</p>");
}
</script>

</body>
</html>
```

This is a heading

This is a paragraph.

This is another paragraph.

Figure 2.2

The preceding example is not very useful. It just demonstrates the use of a block. Normally, a block is used to group statements together in a function or in a condition (in which a group of statements should be executed if a condition is met).

You will learn more about functions and conditions in Chapters 6 and 10.

JavaScript Comments

JavaScript comments can be added to explain the JavaScript script or to make the code more readable.

Single line comments start with //.

The following example uses single-line comments to explain the code.

Your result is shown in Figure 2.3.

```
<html>
<body>

<script type="text/javascript">
// Write a heading
document.write("<h1>This is a heading</h1>");
// Write two paragraphs:
document.write("<p>This is a paragraph.</p>");
document.write("<p>This is another paragraph.</p>");
</script>

</body>
</html>
```

This is a heading

This is a paragraph.

This is another paragraph.

Figure 2.3

JavaScript Multiline Comments

Multiline comments start with /* and end with */.

The following example uses a multiline comment to explain the code.

Your result is shown in Figure 2.4.

```
<html>
<body>

<script type="text/javascript">
```

(continued)

(continued)

```
/*
The code below will write
one heading and two paragraphs
*/
document.write("<h1>This is a heading</h1>");
document.write("<p>This is a paragraph.</p>");
document.write("<p>This is another paragraph.</p>");
</script>

</body>
</html>
```

Figure 2.4

Using Comments to Prevent Execution

In the following example, the comment is used to prevent the execution of a single code line (can be suitable for debugging):

Your result is shown in Figure 2.5.

Try it yourself >>

```
<html>
<body>

<script type="text/javascript">
//document.write("<h1>This is a heading</h1>");
document.write("<p>This is a paragraph.</p>");
document.write("<p>This is another paragraph.</p>");
```

```
</script>

</body>
</html>
```

```
This is a paragraph.

This is another paragraph.
```

Figure 2.5

In the following example, the comment is used to prevent the execution of a code block (can be suitable for debugging):

```
<html>
<body>

<script type="text/javascript">
/*
document.write("<h1>This is a heading</h1>");
document.write("<p>This is a paragraph.</p>");
document.write("<p>This is another paragraph.</p>");
*/
</script>

</body>
</html>
```

Your result would be a blank screen.

Using Comments at the End of a Line

In the following example, the comment is placed at the end of a code line. Your result is shown in Figure 2.6.

```html
<html>
<body>

<script type="text/javascript">
document.write("Hello"); // Write "Hello"
document.write(" Dolly!"); // Write " Dolly!"
</script>

</body>
</html>
```

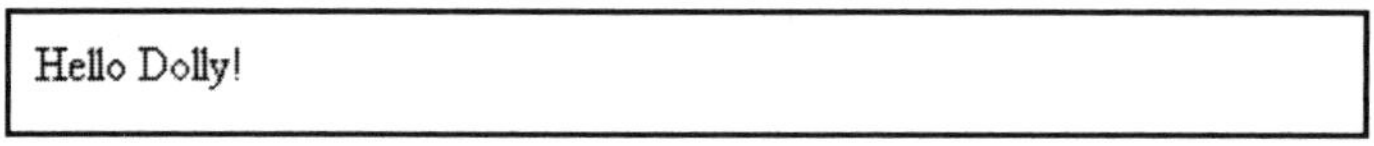

Hello Dolly!

Figure 2.6

CHAPTER 3

JAVASCRIPT VARIABLES

In This Chapter

- ❏ Do You Remember Algebra from School?
- ❏ JavaScript Variables
- ❏ Declaring (Creating) JavaScript Variables
- ❏ Assigning Values to Undeclared JavaScript Variables
- ❏ Redeclaring JavaScript Variables
- ❏ JavaScript Arithmetic

Variables are "containers" for storing information.

Do You Remember Algebra from School?

Do you remember algebra from school?

$x = 5, y = 6, z = x + y$

Do you remember that a letter (like x) could be used to hold a value (like 5), and that you could use the information given to calculate the value of z to be 11?

These letters are called **variables**. Variables can be used to hold values ($x = 5$) or expressions ($z = x + y$).

JavaScript Variables

As with algebra, JavaScript variables are used to hold values or expressions. A variable can have a short name, like x, or a more descriptive name, like *carname*.

Rules for JavaScript variable names:

▸▸ Variable names are case sensitive (*y* and *Y* are two different variables).

▸▸ Variable names must begin with a letter, the underscore character, or a dollar sign. (The $ character is used primarily by code-generation tools.)

▸▸ Subsequent characters may be letter, number, underscore, or dollar sign.

N O T E There are 59 reserved words that are not legal variable names.

T I P Because JavaScript is case sensitive, variable names are case sensitive.

A variable's value can change during the execution of a script. You can refer to a variable by its name to display or change its value. Your result is shown in Figure 3.1.

Try it yourself >>

```html
<html>
<body>

<script type="text/javascript">
var firstname;
firstname="Hege";
document.write(firstname);
document.write("<br />");
firstname="Tove";
document.write(firstname);
</script>

<p>The script above declares a variable,
assigns a value to it, displays the value, changes the
   value,and displays the value again.</p>

</body>
</html>
```

```
Hege
Tove

The script above declares a variable, assigns a value to it, displays the value,
changes the value, and displays the value again.
```

Figure 3.1

Declaring (Creating) JavaScript Variables

Creating variables in JavaScript is most often referred to as "declaring" variables.

You can declare JavaScript variables with the var statement:

```
var x;
var carname;
```

After the declaration shown, the variables are empty. (They have no values yet.) However, you can also assign values to the variables when you declare them:

```
var x=5;
var carname="Volvo";
```

After the execution of the preceding statements, the variable *x* will hold the value **5**, and *carname* will hold the value **Volvo**.

> **NOTE** When you assign a text value to a variable, use quotes around the value.

Assigning Values to Undeclared JavaScript Variables

If you assign values to variables that have not yet been declared, the variables will automatically be declared.

The following statements:

```
x=5;
carname="Volvo";
```

(continued)

(continued)

have the same effect as these:

```
var x=5;
var carname="Volvo";
```

Redeclaring JavaScript Variables

If you redeclare a JavaScript variable, it will not lose its original value.

```
var x=5;
var x;
```

After the execution of the preceding statements, the variable *x* will still have the value of 5. The value of *x* is not reset (or cleared) when you redeclare it.

JavaScript Arithmetic

As with algebra, you can do arithmetic operations with JavaScript variables:

```
y=x-5;
z=y+5;
```

NOTE Sometimes the results seem unpredictable. If at least one variable on the right side of an assignment expression contains a string value, the result will be a string and the "+" operator is applied as the concatenation operator to the toString() values of the variables. Only if all the variables to the right of the assignment operator are numbers will the result be a number.

You will learn more about the operators that can be used in Chapter 4, "JavaScript Operators."

JAVASCRIPT OPERATORS

In This Chapter

❑ JavaScript Arithmetic Operators

❑ JavaScript Assignment Operators

❑ The + Operator Used on Strings

❑ Adding Strings and Numbers

The assignment operator, =, is used to assign values to JavaScript variables, as shown in the first two lines of the following code.

The arithmetic operator, +, is used to add values together, as shown in the last line of the following code.

```
y = 5;
z = 2;
x = y+z;
```

The value of x, after the execution of the preceding statements is 7.

JavaScript Arithmetic Operators

Arithmetic operators are used to perform arithmetic between variables and/or values.

Given that $y = 5$, the following table explains the arithmetic operators.

Operator	Description	Example	Result
+	Addition	x = y+2	x = 7
-	Subtraction	x = y-2	x = 3
*	Multiplication	x = y*2	x = 10
/	Division	x = y/2	x = 2.5
%	Modulus (division remainder)	x = y%2	x = 1
++	Increment	x = ++y	x = 6
--	Decrement	x = --y	x = 4

JavaScript Assignment Operators

Assignment operators are used to assign values to JavaScript variables.

Given that $x = 10$ and $y = 5$, the following table explains the assignment operators:

Operator	Example	Same As	Result
=	x = y		x = 5
+=	x+ = y	x = x+y	x = 15
-=	x- = y	x = x-y	x = 5
*=	x* = y	x = x*y	x = 50
/=	x/ = y	x = x/y	x = 2
%=	x% = y	x = x%y	x = 0

The + Operator Used on Strings

The + operator also can be used to concatenate string variables or text values together. To concatenate two or more string variables together, use the + operator:

```
txt1="What a very";
txt2="nice day";
txt3=txt1+txt2;
```

After the execution of the preceding statements, the variable `txt3` contains "What a verynice day".

To add a space between the two strings, insert a space into one of the strings:

```
txt1="What a very ";
txt2="nice day";
txt3=txt1+txt2;
```

Or insert a space into the expression:

```
txt1="What a very";
txt2="nice day";
txt3=txt1+" "+txt2;
```

After the execution of the preceding statements, the variable `txt3` contains:

"What a very nice day"

Adding Strings and Numbers

The rule is as follows:

If you add a number and a string, the result will be a string! Your results are shown in Figure 4.1.

Try it yourself >>

```
<html>
<body>

<script type="text/javascript">
x=5+5;
document.write(x);
document.write("<br />");
x="5"+"5";
document.write(x);
document.write("<br />");
x=5+"5";
document.write(x);
document.write("<br />");
x="5"+5;
document.write(x);
document.write("<br />");
</script>

<p>The rule is: If you add a number and a string, the result
   will be a string.</p>

</body>
</html>
```

```
10
55
55
55

The rule is: If you add a number and a string, the result will be a string.
```

Figure 4.1

CHAPTER 5

JAVASCRIPT COMPARISONS

In This Chapter

❏ Comparison Operators

❏ How to Use Comparisons

❏ Logical Operators

❏ Conditional Operator

Comparison and logical operators are used to test for true or false.

Comparison Operators

Comparison operators are used in logical statements to determine equality or difference between variables or values.

Given that $x = 5$, the following table explains the comparison operators:

Operator	Description	Example
==	is equal to value...is equal to value	x == 8 is false
===	is exactly equal to value and type	x === 5 is true
		x === "5" is false
!=	is not equal	x! = 8 is true
>	is greater than	x > 8 is false
<	is less than	x < 8 is true
>=	is greater than or equal to	x >= 8 is false
<=	is less than or equal to	x <= 8 is true

How to Use Comparisons

Comparison operators can be used in conditional statements to compare values and take action depending on the result:

```
if (age<18) document.write("Too young");
```

You will learn more about the use of conditional statements in the next chapter.

Logical Operators

Logical operators are used to determine the logic between variables or values.

Given that $x = 6$ and $y = 3$, the following table explains the logical operators:

Operator	Description	Example
&&	and	(x < 10 && y > 1) is true
||	or	(x == 5 || y == 5) is false
!	not	!(x == y) is true

Conditional Operator

JavaScript also contains a conditional operator that assigns a value to a variable based on some condition. The syntax is as follows:

```
variablename=(condition)?value1:value2
```

For example,

```
greeting=(visitor=="PRES")?"Dear President ":"Dear ";
```

If the variable *visitor* has the value of "PRES", then the variable *greeting* will be assigned the value "Dear President " else it will be assigned "Dear".

CHAPTER 6

JAVASCRIPT IF...ELSE STATEMENTS

In This Chapter

❑ Conditional Statements

❑ if Statement

❑ if...else Statement

❑ if...else if...else Statement

Conditional statements are used to perform different actions based on different conditions.

Conditional Statements

Very often when you write code, you want to perform different actions for different decisions. You can use conditional statements in your code to do this.

JavaScript has the following conditional statements:

▸▸ **if statement.** Use this statement to execute some code only if a specified condition is true.

▸▸ **if...else statement.** Use this statement to execute some code if the condition is true and another code if the condition is false.

▸▸ **if...else if....else statement.** Use this statement to select one of many blocks of code to be executed.

▸▸ **switch statement.** Use this statement to select one of many blocks of code to be executed.

> **TIP** With conditionals, a { } block must contain the statements to be executed. If curly braces are not present, only the subsequent statement is executed, which is a very common programming error.
>
> ```
> if (condition)
>    {
>       statement 1;
>       statement 2;
>       statement 3;
>    } // all three statements are executed
>
>
> if (condition)
>     statement 1;
>     statement 2;
>     statement 3;
>      // only statement 1 is executed
> ```

if Statement

Use the if statement to execute some code only if a specified condition is true.

The syntax is as follows:

```
if (condition)
   {
   code to be executed if condition is true
   }
```

Your result is shown in Figure 6.1.

> **TIP** if is written in lowercase letters. Using uppercase letters (IF) will generate a JavaScript error!

Try it yourself >>

```
<html>
<body>

<script type="text/javascript">
var d = new Date();
var time = d.getHours();
```

(continued)

(continued)

```
if (time < 10)
  {
  document.write("<b>Good morning</b>");
  }
</script>

<p>This example demonstrates the If statement.</p>
<p>If the time on your browser is less than 10, you will get
  a "Good morning" greeting.</p>

</body>
</html>
```

This example demonstrates the If statement.

If the time on your browser is less than 10, you will get a "Good morning" greeting.

Figure 6.1

NOTE There is no ..else.. in this syntax. You tell the browser to execute some code only if the specified condition is true.

if...else Statement

Use the if....else statement to execute some code if a condition is true and another code if the condition is not true.

The syntax is as follows:

```
if (condition)
  {
  code to be executed if condition is true
  }
else
  {
  code to be executed if condition is not true
  }
```

Try it yourself >>

```
<html>
<body>

<script type="text/javascript">
var d = new Date();
var time = d.getHours();

if (time < 10)
{
document.write("<b>Good morning</b>");
}
else
{
document.write("<b>Good day</b>");
}
</script>

<p>
This example demonstrates the If...Else statement.
</p>

<p>
If the time on your browser is less than 10,
you will get a "Good morning" greeting.
Otherwise you will get a "Good day" greeting.
</p>

</body>
</html>
```

Your result is shown in Figure 6.2.

Good day

This example demonstrates the If...Else statement.

If the time on your browser is less than 10, you will get a "Good morning" greeting. Otherwise you will get a "Good day" greeting.

Figure 6.2

The following example demonstrates a random link. When you click on the link, it will take you to w3schools.com OR to RefsnesData.no. There is a 50 percent chance for each of them. Your result is shown in Figure 6.3.

```
<html>
<body>

<script type="text/javascript">
var r=Math.random();
if (r>0.5)
{
document.write("<a href='http://www.w3schools.com'>Learn Web
    Development!</a>");
}
else
{
document.write("<a href='http://www.refsnesdata.no'>Visit
    Refsnes Data!</a>");
}
</script>

</body>
</html>
```

Learn Web Development!

Figure 6.3

if...else if...else Statement

Use the if....else if...else statement to select one of several blocks of code to be executed.

The syntax is as follows:

```
if (condition1)
  {
  code to be executed if condition1 is true
```

```
}
else if (condition2)
  {
  code to be executed if condition2 is true
  }
else
  {
  code to be executed if condition1 and condition2 are not
  true
  }
```

Your result is shown in Figure 6.4.

Try it yourself >>

```
<html>
<body>

<script type="text/javascript">
var d = new Date();
var time = d.getHours();
if (time<10)
{
document.write("<b>Good morning</b>");
}
else if (time>=10 && time<16)
{
document.write("<b>Good day</b>");
}
else
{
document.write("<b>Hello World!</b>");
}
</script>

<p>
This example demonstrates the if..else if...else statement.
</p>
```

(continued)

37

(continued)

```
        </body>
        </html>
```

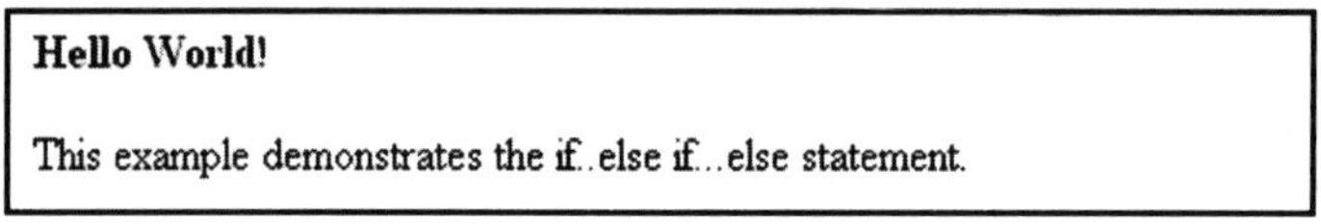

Hello World!

This example demonstrates the if..else if...else statement.

Figure 6.2

CHAPTER 7

JAVASCRIPT LOOPS

In This Chapter

❏ The for Loop

❏ The while Loop

❏ The do...while Loop

Loops execute a block of code a specified number of times or while a specified condition is true.

Often when you write code, you want the same block of code to run over and over again in a row. Instead of adding several almost equal lines in a script, you can use loops to perform a task like this.

In JavaScript, there are two kinds of loops:

▸▸ **for.** Loops through a block of code a specified number of times

▸▸ **while.** Loops through a block of code while a specified condition is true

The for Loop

The for loop is used when you know in advance how many times the script should run.

The syntax is as follows:

```
for (var=startvalue;var<=endvalue;var=var+increment)
{
code to be executed
}
```

The following example defines a loop that starts with i = 0. The loop will continue to run as long as *i* is less than or equal to 5. *i* will increase by 1 each time the loop runs. Your result is shown in Figure 7.1.

> **NOTE** The increment parameter could also be negative, and the <= could be any comparing statement.

```html
<html>
<body>

<script type="text/javascript">
for (i = 0; i <= 5; i++)
{
document.write("The number is " + i);
document.write("<br />");
}
</script>

<p>Explanation:</p>

<p>This for loop starts with i=0.</p>

<p>As long as <b>i</b> is less than, or equal to 5, the loop
    will continue to run.</p>

<p><b>i</b> will increase by 1 each time the loop runs.</p>

</body>
</html>
```

The number is 0
The number is 1
The number is 2
The number is 3
The number is 4
The number is 5

Explanation:

This for loop starts with i=0.

As long as i is less than, or equal to 5, the loop will continue to run.

i will increase by 1 each time the loop runs.

Figure 7.1

In the following example, you loop through the six different HTML headings. Your result is shown in Figure 7.2.

```
<html>
<body>

<script type="text/javascript">
for (i = 1; i <= 6; i++)
{
document.write("<h" + i + ">This is heading " + i);
document.write("</h" + i + ">");
}
</script>

</body>
</html>
```

This is heading 1

This is heading 2

This is heading 3

This is heading 4

This is heading 5

This is heading 6

Figure 7.2

The while Loop

The `while` loop loops through a block of code a specified number of times or while a specified condition is true.

The syntax is as follows:

```
while (var<=endvalue)
  {
```

(continued)

(continued)
```
        code to be executed
        }
```

> **N O T E** The <= could be any comparing statement.

> **T I P** The distinction between the `for` and the `while` is that in the `for` loop, the conditions are known and can be specified beforehand. The `while` loop is used when the initial conditions are known, but the terminal condition is discovered as the block is executed.

The following example defines a loop that starts with `i = 0`. The loop will continue to run as long as *i* is less than or equal to 5. *i* will increase by 1 each time the loop runs, as shown in Figure 7.3.

Try it yourself >>

```
<html>
<body>

<script type="text/javascript">
i=0;
while (i<=5)
{
document.write("The number is " + i);
document.write("<br />");
i++;
}
</script>

<p>Explanation:</p>
<p><b>i</b> is equal to 0.</p>
<p>While <b>i</b> is less than, or equal to, 5, the loop
   will continue to run.</p>
<p><b>i</b> will increase by 1 each time the loop runs.</p>

</body>
</html>
```

The number is 0
The number is 1
The number is 2
The number is 3
The number is 4
The number is 5

Explanation:

i is equal to 0.

While **i** is less than, or equal to, 5, the loop will continue to run.

i will increase by 1 each time the loop runs.

Figure 7.3

The do...while Loop

The `do...while` loop is a variant of the `while` loop. This loop will execute the block of code *once*, and then it will repeat the loop as long as the specified condition is true.

The syntax is as follows:

```
do
  {
  code to be executed
  }
while (var<=endvalue);
```

The following example uses a `do...while` loop. The `do...while` loop will always be executed at least once, even if the condition is false, because the statements are executed before the condition is tested. The result is shown in Figure 7.4.

> **TIP** The difference between the `while` and `do...while` loops should be characterized by whether the condition is checked before or after the block is executed. In the case of the `while` loop, the condition is checked first, so if false, the block will not be executed. In the `do...while` loop, the condition is checked **after** the block is executed; therefore the block is always executed at least once.

43

Learn JavaScript and Ajax with w3schools

Try it yourself >>

```html
<html>
<body>

<script type="text/javascript">
i = 0;
do
{
document.write("The number is " + i);
document.write("<br />");
i++;
}
while (i <= 5)
</script>

<p>Explanation:</p>

<p><b>i</b>  equal to 0.</p>

<p>The loop will run</p>

<p><b>i</b> will increase by 1 each time the loop runs.</p>

<p>While <b>i</b> is less than, or equal to, 5, the loop
  will continue to run.</p>


</body>
</html>
```

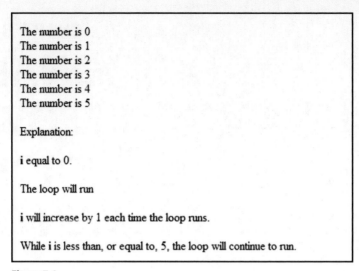

The number is 0
The number is 1
The number is 2
The number is 3
The number is 4
The number is 5

Explanation:

i equal to 0.

The loop will run

i will increase by 1 each time the loop runs.

While i is less than, or equal to, 5, the loop will continue to run.

Figure 7.4

CHAPTER 8

ADDITIONAL JAVASCRIPT FLOW CONTROL STATEMENTS

In This Chapter

- ❑ The **break** Statement
- ❑ The **continue** Statement
- ❑ JavaScript **for...in** Statement
- ❑ JavaScript **switch** Statement

The **break** and **continue** statements are used to control loop execution. The **break** statement can be used to halt execution of a loop if, for example, an error condition is encountered. The **continue** statement is used to begin the next iteration of a loop without executing all the statements in the block.

The break Statement

The **break** statement will terminate execution of the loop and continue executing the code that follows after the loop (if any). Your result is shown in Figure 8.1.

Try it yourself >>

```
<html>
<body>
<script type="text/javascript">
var i=0;
for (i=0;i<=10;i++)
```

```
{
if (i==3)
  {
  break;
  }
document.write("The number is " + i);
document.write("<br />");
}
</script>
<p>Explanation: The loop will break when i=3.</p>
</body>
</html>
```

```
The number is 0
The number is 1
The number is 2

Explanation: The loop will break when i=3.
```

Figure 8.1

The continue Statement

The continue statement will terminate the current iteration and restart the loop with the next value. Your result is shown in Figure 8.2.

Try it yourself >>

```
<html>
<body>
<script type="text/javascript">
var i=0;
for (i=0;i<=10;i++)
{
if (i==3)
  {
  continue;
  }
document.write("The number is " + i);
document.write("<br />");
```

(continued)

47

(continued)

```
    }
    </script>

    <p>Explanation: The loop will break the current loop and
       continue with the next value when i=3.</p>

    </body>
    </html>
```

```
The number is 0
The number is 1
The number is 2
The number is 4
The number is 5
The number is 6
The number is 7
The number is 8
The number is 9
The number is 10

Explanation: The loop will break the current loop and continue with the
next value when i=3.
```

Figure 8.2

JavaScript for...in Statement

The for...in statement loops through the elements of an array or through the properties of an object.

The syntax is as follows:

```
for (variable in object)
  {
  code to be executed
  }
```

> **NOTE** The code in the body of the for...in loop is executed once for each element/property.

> **NOTE** The variable argument can be a named variable, an array element, or a property of an object.

 Arrays are discussed more fully in Chapter 17, "JavaScript Array Object."

In the following example, use the for...in statement to loop through an array. Your result is shown in Figure 8.3.

Try it yourself >>

```
<html>
<body>
<script type="text/javascript">
var x;
var mycars = new Array();
mycars[0] = "Saab";
mycars[1] = "Volvo";
mycars[2] = "BMW";

for (x in mycars)
{
document.write(mycars[x] + "<br />");
}
</script>
</body>
</html>
```

```
Saab
Volvo
BMW
```

Figure 8.3

Conditional statements are used to perform different actions based on different conditions.

JavaScript switch Statement

Use the `switch` statement to select one of many blocks of code to be executed.

The syntax is as follows:

```
switch(n)
{
case 1:
  execute code block 1
  break;
case 2:
  execute code block 2
  break;
default:
  code to be executed if n is different from case 1 and 2
}
```

This is how it works: First we have a single expression *n* (most often a variable) that is evaluated once. The value of the expression is then compared with the values for each case in the structure. If there is a match, the block of code associated with that case is executed.

Execution continues until either the end of the switch block is reached or a **break** statement is encountered. For example:

```
<html>
<body>
<script type="text/javascript">
var i = 1;
switch (i)
{
case 0:
    document.write("<b>i == 0</b><br>");
case 1:
    document.write("<b>i == 1</b><br>");
case 2:
    document.write("<b>i == 2</b><br>");
    break;
case 3:
    document.write("<b>i == 3</b><br>");
    break;
```

```
default:
    document.write("<b>i > 3</b><br>");
}
</script>
<p>Note that when i == 1 execution begins with case 1: but
    continues until the break statement is encountered.</>
</body>
</html>
```

Your results are shown in Figure 8.4.

Try it yourself >>

```
<html>
<body>
<script type="text/javascript">
var d = new Date();
theDay=d.getDay();
switch (theDay)
{
case 5:
  document.write("<b>Finally Friday</b>");
  break;
case 6:
  document.write("<b>Super Saturday</b>");
  break;
case 0:
  document.write("<b>Sleepy Sunday</b>");
  break;
default:
  document.write("<b>I'm really looking forward to this
  weekend!</b>");
}
</script>

<p>This JavaScript will generate a different greeting based
  on what day it is. Note that Sunday=0, Monday=1, Tues-
  day=2, etc.</p>
```

(continued)

51

(continued)
```
</body>
</html>
```

Super Saturday

This JavaScript will generate a different greeting based on what day it is.
Note that Sunday=0, Monday=1, Tuesday=2, etc.

Figure 8.4

CHAPTER 9

JAVASCRIPT POPUP BOXES

In This Chapter

❑ Popup Boxes

- Alert Box
- Confirm Box
- Prompt Box

Popup Boxes

JavaScript has three types of popup boxes: alert box, confirm box, and prompt box.

Alert Box

An alert box is often used when you want to display information to the user.

When an alert box pops up, the user will have to click OK to proceed.

The syntax is as follows:

```
alert("sometext");
```

Your results are shown in Figure 9.1. When you click the button, the alert box in Figure 9.2 pops up.

Try it yourself >>

```
<html>
<head>
```

(continued)

(continued)

```
<script type="text/javascript">
function show_alert()
{
alert("Hello! I am an alert box!");
}
</script>
</head>
<body>

<input type="button" onclick="show_alert()" value="Show
  alert box" />

</body>
</html>
```

Show alert box

Figure 9.1

Figure 9.2

The following example creates an alert box with line breaks.

Your results are shown in Figures 9.3 and 9.4.

Try it yourself >>

```
<html>
<head>
<script type="text/javascript">
function disp_alert()
{
alert("Hello again! This is how we" + '\n' + "add line
  breaks to an alert box!");
}
```

```
</script>
</head>
<body>

<input type="button" onclick="disp_alert()" value="Display
  alert box" />

</body>
</html>
```

Figure 9.3

Figure 9.4

Confirm Box

A confirm box is often used if you want the user to verify or accept something.

When a confirm box pops up, the user will have to click either OK or Cancel to proceed.

If the user clicks OK, the box returns *true*. If the user clicks Cancel, the box returns *false*.

The syntax is as follows:

```
confirm("sometext");
```

Your results are shown in Figures 9.5 and 9.6.

Try it yourself >>

```
<html>
<head>
<script type="text/javascript">
function show_confirm()
{
```

(continued)

55

(continued)

```
      var r=confirm("Press a button!");
      if (r==true)
        {
        alert("You pressed OK!");
        }
      else
        {
        alert("You pressed Cancel!");
        }
      }
      </script>
      </head>
      <body>

      <input type="button" onclick="show_confirm()" value="Show a
        confirm box" />

      </body>
      </html>
```

Show a confirm box

Figure 9.5

Figure 9.6

Prompt Box

A prompt box is often used if you want the user to input a value while on a page or from a page.

When a prompt box pops up, the user will have to click either OK or Cancel to proceed after entering an input value.

If the user clicks OK, the box returns the input value. If the user clicks Cancel, the box returns null.

The syntax is as follows:

```
prompt("sometext","defaultvalue");
```

Your results are shown in Figure 9.7.

Try it yourself >>

```
<html>
<head>
<script type="text/javascript">
function disp_prompt()
{
var fname=prompt("Please enter your name:","Your name")
document.getElementById("msg").innerHTML="Greetings, " +
   fname
}
</script>
</head>
<body>

<input type="button" onclick="disp_prompt()" value="Display
  a prompt box" />
<br /><br />

<div id="msg"></div>

</body>
</html>
```

```
    Display a prompt box
```

Figure 9.7

CHAPTER 10

JAVASCRIPT FUNCTIONS

In This Chapter

- ❏ How to Define a Function
- ❏ JavaScript Function Examples
- ❏ The `return` Statement
- ❏ The Lifetime of JavaScript Variables

A function will be executed by an event or by an explicit call to the function.

To keep the browser from executing a script when the page loads, you can put your script into a function.

A function contains code that will be executed by an event or by a call to the function.

You may call a function from anywhere within a page (or even from other pages if the function is embedded in an external .js file).

Functions can be defined both in the `<head>` and in the `<body>` section of a document. However, to ensure that a function is read/loaded by the browser before it is called, it should be placed in the `<head>` section.

How to Define a Function

The syntax is as follows:

```
function functionname(var1,var2,...,varX)
{
some code
}
```

The parameters *var1*, *var2*, and so on, are variables or values passed into the function. The { and the } defines the start and end of the function.

> **NOTE** A function with no parameters must include the parentheses () after the function name.

> **TIP** Do not forget about the importance of capitalization in JavaScript! The word function must be written in lowercase letters, otherwise a JavaScript error occurs. Also note that you must call a function with the exact same capitalization as in the function declaration.

JavaScript Function Examples

In the following example, if the line `alert("Hello world!!")` had not been put within a function, it would have been executed as soon as the line was loaded. Now, the script will not be executed before a user clicks the input button. The function `displaymessage()` will be executed if the input button is clicked.

Your results are shown in Figures 10.1 and 10.2.

Try it yourself >>

```
<html>
<head>
<script type="text/javascript">
function displaymessage()
{
alert("Hello World!");
}
</script>
</head>

<body>
<form>
<input type="button" value="Click me!"
  onclick="displaymessage()" />
</form>

<p>By pressing the button above, a function will be called.
  The function will alert a message.</p>
```

(continued)

(continued)
```
</body>
</html>
```

By pressing the button above, a function will be called. The function will alert a message.

Figure 10.1

Figure 10.2

You will learn more about JavaScript events in the Chapter 11, "JavaScript Events."

The following example of a function with a parameter shows how to pass a variable to a function and use the variable in the function.

Your results are shown in Figures 10.3 and 10.4.

Try it yourself >>

```html
<html>
<head>
<script type="text/javascript">
function myfunction(txt)
{
alert(txt);
}
</script>
</head>
<body>

<form>
<input type="button" onclick="myfunction('Hello')"
value="Call function">
</form>
```

60

```
<p>By pressing the button above, a function will be called
   with "Hello" as a parameter. The function will alert the
   parameter.</p>

</body>
</html>
```

Call function

By pressing the button above, a function will be called with "Hello" as a parameter. The function will alert the parameter.

Figure 10.3

Message from webpage

Hello

OK

Figure 10.4

The following example shows how to let a function return a value.

Your results are shown in Figure 10.5

Try it yourself >>

```
<html>
<head>
<script type="text/javascript">
function myFunction()
{
return ("Hello world!");
}
</script>
</head>
<body>

<script type="text/javascript">
document.write(myFunction())
</script>
```

(continued)

(continued)

```
</body>
</html>
```

Hello world!

Figure 10.5

The return Statement

The `return` statement is used to specify the value that is returned from the function.

So, functions that are going to return a value must use the `return` statement.

A `return` statement also may be used in a function that does not return a value to end execution at any given point in the function; for example, if an error condition is encountered:

```
var globalName;
function setGlobalName(name)
{
    if (name.length == 0)
{
Alert("no name specified")
return;
        }
    globalName = name;
    }
```

The following example returns the product of two numbers (*a* and *b*).

Your results are shown in Figure 10.6.

Try it yourself >>

```
<html>
<head>
<script type="text/javascript">
function product(a,b)
{
return a*b;
```

```
}
</script>
</head>

<body>
<script type="text/javascript">
document.write(product(4,3));
</script>

<p>The script in the body section calls a function with two
   parameters (4 and 3).</p>
<p>The function will return the product of these two param-
   eters.</p>
</body>
</html>
```

12

The script in the body section calls a function with two parameters (4 and 3).

The function will return the product of these two parameters.

Figure 10.6

The Lifetime of JavaScript Variables

If you declare a variable within a function, the variable can be accessed only within that function. When you exit the function, the variable is destroyed. These variables are called **local variables.** You can have local variables with the same name in different functions, because each is recognized only by the function in which it is declared.

If you declare a variable outside a function, all the functions on your page can access it. These variables are called **global variables.**

The lifetime of these variables starts when they are declared and ends when the page is closed.

CHAPTER 11

JAVASCRIPT EVENTS

In This Chapter

- ❏ onLoad and onUnload
- ❏ onFocus, onBlur, and onChange
- ❏ onSubmit
- ❏ onMouseOver and onMouseOut
- ❏ onClick

Events are actions that can be detected by JavaScript.

By using JavaScript, we have the ability to create dynamic Web pages.

Every element on a Web page has certain events that can trigger a JavaScript. For example, we can use the onClick event of a button element to indicate that a function will run when a user clicks the button. We define the events in the HTML tags.

Examples of events:

- ▸▸ A mouse click
- ▸▸ A Web page or an image loading
- ▸▸ Mousing over a hot spot on the Web page
- ▸▸ Selecting an input field in an HTML form
- ▸▸ Submitting an HTML form

> **NOTE** Events are normally used in combination with functions, and the function will not be executed before the event occurs!

onLoad and onUnload

The onLoad and onUnload events are triggered when the user enters or leaves the page.

The onLoad event is often used to check the visitor's browser type and browser version and load the proper version of the Web page based on the information.

Both the onLoad and onUnload events often are used to deal with cookies that should be set when a user enters or leaves a page. For example, you could have a popup asking for the user's name upon his first arrival to your page. The name is then stored in a cookie. Next time the visitor arrives at your page, you could have another popup saying something like: "Welcome John Doe!".

onFocus, onBlur, and onChange

The onFocus, onBlur, and onChange events are often used in combination with validation of form fields.

The onFocus and onBlur events are complementary and are caused by the user clicking outside of the current window, frame, or form element or using the Tab key to move among fields or elements. When the user leaves an element, that element triggers a blur event. When the user moves to a new element, that element triggers a focus event.

Following is an example of how to use the onChange event. The checkEmail() function will be called whenever the user changes the content of the field:

```
<input type="text" size="30" id="email"
   onchange="checkEmail()">
```

onSubmit

The onSubmit event may be used to validate form fields before submitting the form.

> TIP Because the programmer controls the function executed on onSubmit, he can validate any, all, or no inputs as he sees fit.

Following is an example of how to use the onSubmit event. The checkForm() function will be called when the user clicks the Submit button in the form. If the field values are not accepted, the submit should be cancelled. The function checkForm() returns either *true* or *false*. If it returns true, the form will be submitted, otherwise the submit will be cancelled:

```
<form method="post" action="xxx.htm" onsubmit="return
   checkForm()">
```

onMouseOver and onMouseOut

onMouseOver and onMouseOut often are used to create Rollover buttons.

Following is an example of an onMouseOver event. An alert box appears when an onMouseOver event is detected:

```
<a href="http://www.w3schools.com" onmouseover="alert('An
  onMouseOver event');return false"><img src="w3s.gif"
  alt="w3schools" /></a>
```

onClick

The onClick event occurs when the user mouse clicks on a visible element on the screen. The following example could be used to translate text on a page when requested by the user:

```
<input type="button" name="language" value="Click for
  Spanish" onclick="translate()">
```

CHAPTER 12

JAVASCRIPT TRY...CATCH AND THROW STATEMENTS

In This Chapter

- ❑ JavaScript—Catching Errors
- ❑ The `try...catch` Statement
- ❑ The `throw` Statement

The `try...catch` statement enables you to trap errors that occur during the execution of a block of code.

JavaScript—Catching Errors

When browsing Web pages on the Internet, we all have seen a JavaScript alert box telling us there is a runtime error and asking "Do you wish to debug?" Error messages like this may be useful for developers but not for users. When users see errors, they often leave the Web page.

This chapter teaches you how to catch and handle JavaScript error messages so you don't lose your audience.

The try...catch Statement

The `try...catch` statement enables you to trap errors that occur during the execution of a block of code. The try block contains the code to be run, and the catch block contains the code to be executed if an error occurs.

The syntax is as follows:

```
try
  {
  //Run some code here
  }
catch(err)
  {
  //Handle errors here
  }
```

NOTE Note that try...catch is written in lowercase letters. Using uppercase letters will generate a JavaScript error!

The following example is supposed to alert "Welcome guest!" when the button is clicked. However, there's a typo in the message() function. alert() is misspelled as adddlert(). A JavaScript error occurs. The catch block catches the error and executes a custom code to handle it. The code displays a custom error message informing the user what happened. Your results are shown in Figures 12.1 and 12.2.

Try it yourself >>

```
<html>
<head>
<script type="text/javascript">
var txt="";
function message()
{
try
  {
  adddlert("Welcome guest!");
  }
catch(err)
  {
  txt="There was an error on this page.\n\n";
  txt+="Error message: " + err.message + "\n\n";
  txt+="Click OK to continue.\n\n";
  alert(txt);
  }
}
</script>
</head>
```

```
<body>
<input type="button" value="View message" onclick="message()"
  />
</body>

</html>
```

```
View message
```

Figure 12.1

Figure 12.2

The next example uses a confirm box to display a custom message telling users they can click OK to continue viewing the page or click Cancel to go to the homepage. If the confirm method returns *false*, the user clicked Cancel, and the code redirects the user. If the confirm method returns true, the code does nothing. Your results are shown in Figures 12.3 and 12.4.

Try it yourself >>

```
<html>
<head>
<script type="text/javascript">
var txt="";
function message()
{
try
  {
  adddlert("Welcome guest!");
  }
catch(err)
  {
```

(continued)

(continued)

```
      txt="There was an error on this page.\n\n";
      txt+="Click OK to continue viewing this page,\n";
      txt+="or Cancel to return to the home page.\n\n";
      if(!confirm(txt))
        {
        document.location.href="http://www.w3schools.com/";
        }
      }
    }
</script>
</head>

<body>
<input type="button" value="View message" onclick="message()"
  />
</body>

</html>
```

Figure 12.3

Figure 12.4

The throw Statement

The throw statement allows you to create an exception. If you use this statement together with the try...catch statement, you can control program flow and generate accurate error messages.

The syntax is as follows:

```
throw(exception)
```

The exception can be a string, integer, Boolean, or an object.

NOTE throw is written in lowercase letters. Using uppercase letters will generate a JavaScript error!

The following example determines the value of a variable called *x*. If the value of *x* is higher than 10, lower than 0, or not a number, we are going to throw an error. The error is then caught by the catch argument, and the proper error message is displayed:

```
<html>
<body>
<script type="text/javascript">
var x=prompt("Enter a number between 0 and 10:","");
try
{
if(x>10)
  {
  throw "Err1";
  }
else if(x<0)
  {
  throw "Err2";
  }
else if(isNaN(x))
  {
  throw "Err3";
  }
}
catch(er)
{
if(er=="Err1")
  {
  alert("Error! The value is too high");
  }
if(er=="Err2")
  {
  alert("Error! The value is too low");
```

(continued)

71

(continued)

```
        }
    if(er=="Err3")
      {
      alert("Error! The value is not a number");
      }
    }
    </script>
    </body>
    </html>
```

CHAPTER 13

JAVASCRIPT SPECIAL CHARACTERS AND GUIDELINES

In This Chapter

- ❑ Insert Special Characters
- ❑ JavaScript Is Case Sensitive
- ❑ White Space
- ❑ Break up a Code Line

In JavaScript, you can add special characters to a text string by using the backslash character. Also, when scripting with JavaScript, you should know some other important guidelines.

Insert Special Characters

The backslash (\) is used to insert apostrophes, new lines, quotes, and other special characters into a text string.

Look at the following JavaScript code:

```javascript
var txt="We are the so-called "Vikings" from the north.";
document.write(txt);
```

In JavaScript, a string is started and stopped with either single or double quotes. This means that the preceding string will be chopped to *We are the so-called*.

To solve this problem, you must place a backslash (\) before each double quote in "Viking". This turns each double quote into a string literal:

```javascript
var txt="We are the so-called \"Vikings\" from the north.";
document.write(txt);
```

JavaScript will now output the proper text string: *We are the so-called "Vikings" from the north.*

Here is another example:

```
document.write ("You \& I are singing!");
```

The previous example will produce the following output:

```
You & I are singing!
```

The following table lists other special characters that can be added to a text string with the backslash sign:

Code	Outputs
\'	single quote
\"	double quote
\&	ampersand
\\	backslash
\n	new line
\r	carriage return
\t	tab
\b	backspace
\f	form feed

JavaScript Is Case Sensitive

A function named `myfunction` is not the same as `myFunction` and a variable named `myVar` is not the same as `myvar`.

JavaScript is case sensitive; therefore, watch your capitalization closely when you create or call variables, objects, and functions.

White Space

JavaScript ignores extra spaces. You can add white space to your script to make it more readable. The following lines are equivalent:

```
name="Hege";
name = "Hege";
```

Break up a Code Line

Text in code statements contained within quotes is called a **string literal**. A string literal may not be broken across lines except by inserting the backslash character (\) at the point where you want to break the string:

```
document.write("Hello \
World!");
```

The following will generate an "unterminated string literal" script error:

```
document.write("Hello
World!");
```

Another option is to use the concatenate operator (+) to break the string:

```
document.write("Hello "+
"World!");
```

Code statements may be broken across lines, but the backslash character must not be used in this case.

The following is legal JavaScript:

```
document.write
("Hello "
+
World!"
);
```

As a rule, break code statements or string literals across lines only when the length of the line or literal makes it difficult to read.

You can break up a code line **within a text string** with a backslash. The following example will be displayed properly:

```
document.write("Hello \
World!");
```

However, you cannot break up a code line like this:

```
document.write \
("Hello World!");
```

Section II
JavaScript Objects

CHAPTER 14

JAVASCRIPT OBJECTS INTRO

In This Chapter

❑ Object-Oriented Programming

❑ Properties

❑ Methods

JavaScript as a programming language has strong object-oriented capabilities. An Object-Oriented (OOL) language enables you to model data using objects consisting of properties and methods that operate on those properties.

Object-Oriented Programming

Creating your own objects is explained later in the section "Advanced JavaScript." We start by looking at the built-in JavaScript objects and how they are used. The next pages explain each built-in JavaScript object in detail.

Note that an object is just a special kind of data. An object has properties and methods.

Properties

Properties are the values associated with an object.

In the following example, we use the length property of the String object to return the number of characters in a string:

```
<script type="text/javascript">
var txt="Hello World!";
document.write(txt.length);
</script>
```

(continued)

(continued)

The output of the previous code will be

12

Methods

Methods are the actions that can be performed on objects.

In the following example, we use the `toUpperCase()` method of the String object to display a text in uppercase letters:

```
<script type="text/javascript">
var str="Hello world!";
document.write(str.toUpperCase());
</script>
```

The output of the previous code will be

HELLO WORLD!

CHAPTER 15

JAVASCRIPT STRING OBJECT

In This Chapter

❑ String Object

❑ Examples

The String object is used to manipulate a stored piece of text.

String Object

The following example uses the `length` property of the String object to find the length of a string:

```
var txt="Hello world!";
document.write(txt.length);
```

The preceding code will result in the following output:

```
12
```

The following example uses the `toUpperCase()` method of the String object to convert a string to uppercase letters:

```
var txt="Hello world!";
document.write(txt.toUpperCase());
```

The preceding code will result in the following output:

```
HELLO WORLD!
```

Examples

The following example shows how to return the length of a string. Your results are shown in Figure 15.1.

```
<html>
<body>

<script type="text/javascript">

var txt = "Hello World!";
document.write(txt.length);

</script>

</body>
</html>
```

```
12
```

Figure 15.1

The following example demonstrates how to use the methods of the String object to style strings. Your results are shown in Figure 15.2.

```
<html>
<body>

<script type="text/javascript">

var txt = "Hello World!";
```

```
document.write("<p>Big: " + txt.big() + "</p>");
document.write("<p>Small: " + txt.small() + "</p>");

document.write("<p>Bold: " + txt.bold() + "</p>");
document.write("<p>Italic: " + txt.italics() + "</p>");

document.write("<p>Fixed: " + txt.fixed() + "</p>");
document.write("<p>Strike: " + txt.strike() + "</p>");

document.write("<p>Fontcolor: " + txt.fontcolor("green") +
  "</p>");
document.write("<p>Fontsize: " + txt.fontsize(6) + "</p>");

document.write("<p>Subscript: " + txt.sub() + "</p>");
document.write("<p>Superscript: " + txt.sup() + "</p>");

document.write("<p>Link: " + txt.link("http://www.w3schools.
  com") + "</p>");

document.write("<p>Blink: " + txt.blink() + " (does not work
  in IE, Chrome, or Safari)</p>");

</script>

</body>
</html>
```

Big: **Hello World!**

Small: Hello World!

Bold: **Hello World!**

Italic: *Hello World!*

Fixed: `Hello World!`

Strike: ~~Hello World!~~

Fontcolor: Hello World!

Fontsize: Hello World!

Subscript: Hello World!

Superscript: Hello World!

Link: Hello World!

Blink: Hello World! (does not work in IE, Chrome, or Safari)

Figure 15.2

The following example demonstrates conversion of a string to lowercase or uppercase. Your results are shown in Figure 15.3.

Try it yourself >>

```
<html>
<body>

<script type="text/javascript">

var txt="Hello World!";
document.write(txt.toLowerCase() + "<br />");
document.write(txt.toUpperCase());

</script>
```

```
</body>
</html>
```

Your results are shown in Figure 15.3.

```
hello world!
HELLO WORLD!
```

Figure 15.3

The following example demonstrates how to search for a specified value within a string. Your results are shown in Figure 15.4.

Try it yourself >>

```
<html>
<body>

<script type="text/javascript">
var str="Hello world!";
document.write(str.match("world") + "<br />");
document.write(str.match("World") + "<br />");
document.write(str.match("worlld") + "<br />");
document.write(str.match("world!"));
</script>

</body>
</html>
```

```
world
null
null
world!
```

Figure 15.4

The following example shows how to replace a specified value with another value in a string. Your results are shown in Figure 15.5.

```
<html>
<body>

<script type="text/javascript">

var str="Visit Microsoft!";
document.write(str.replace("Microsoft","w3schools"));

</script>
</body>
</html>
```

Visit w3schools!

Figure 15.5

The following example demonstrates how to find the position of the first occurrence of a specified value in a string. Your results are shown in Figure 15.6.

```
<html>
<body>

<script type="text/javascript">
var str="Hello world!";
document.write(str.indexOf("Hello") + "<br />");
document.write(str.indexOf("WORLD") + "<br />");
document.write(str.indexOf("world"));
</script>

</body>
</html>
```

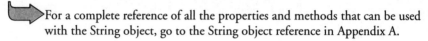

```
0
-1
6
```

Figure 15.6

For a complete reference of all the properties and methods that can be used with the String object, go to the String object reference in Appendix A.

The reference contains a brief description and usage examples for each property and method!

CHAPTER 16

JAVASCRIPT DATE OBJECT

In This Chapter

- ❏ Create a Date Object
- ❏ Set Dates
- ❏ Compare Two Dates
- ❏ Examples

The Date object is used to work with dates and times.

Create a Date Object

The Date object is used to work with dates and times.

Date objects are created with the `Date()` constructor.

There are four ways of instantiating a date:

```
new Date() // current date and time
new Date(milliseconds) //milliseconds since 1970/01/01
new Date(dateString)
new Date(year, month, day, hours, minutes, seconds, milli-
    seconds)
```

Most of the preceding parameters are optional.

When a parameter is not specified, 0 is passed to the method by default.

After a Date object is created, a number of methods enable you to operate on it. Most methods allow you to get and set the year, month, day, hour, minute, second, and millisecond of the object, using either local time or UTC (universal, or GMT) time.

All dates are calculated in milliseconds from 01 January, 1970 00:00:00 Universal Time (UTC) with a day containing 86,400,000 milliseconds.

Some examples of instantiating a date:

```
today = new Date()
d1 = new Date("October 13, 1975 11:13:00")
d2 = new Date(79,5,24)
d3 = new Date(79,5,24,11,33,0)
```

For a complete reference of all the properties and methods that can be used with the Date object, go to the complete Date object reference in Appendix A.

The reference contains a brief description and examples of use for each property and method!

Set Dates

We can easily manipulate the date by using the methods available for the Date object.

In the following example, we set a Date object to a specific date (14th January 2010):

```
var myDate=new Date();
myDate.setFullYear(2010,0,14);
```

And in the following example, we set a Date object to be five days into the future:

```
var myDate=new Date();
myDate.setDate(myDate.getDate()+5);
```

NOTE If adding five days to a date shifts the month or year, the changes are handled automatically by the Date object itself!

Compare Two Dates

The Date object is also used to compare two dates.

The following example compares today's date with the 14th January 2010:

```
var myDate=new Date();
myDate.setFullYear(2010,0,14);
var today = new Date();
if (myDate>today)
  {
```

(continued)

(continued)

```
      alert("Today is before 14th January 2010");
      }
   else
      {
      alert("Today is after 14th January 2010");
      }
```

Examples

The following example demonstrates how to use the Date() method to get today's date. Your results are shown in Figure 16.1.

Try it yourself >>

```
<html>
<body>

<script type="text/javascript">

var d=new Date();
document.write(d);

</script>

</body>
</html>
```

Wed Mar 10 2010 23:01:09 GMT-0500 (Eastern Standard Time)

Figure 16.1

The following example demonstrates how to use getTime() to calculate the milliseconds since 1970.

Your results are shown in Figure 16.2.

Try it yourself >>

```
<html>
<body>
```

```
<script type="text/javascript">
var d=new Date();
document.write(d.getTime() + " milliseconds since
   1970/01/01");
</script>

</body>
</html>
```

1268280218119 milliseconds since 1970/01/01

Figure 16.2

The following example shows how to use setFullYear() to set a specific date. Your results are shown in Figure 16.3.

```
<html>
<body>

<script type="text/javascript">

var d = new Date();
d.setFullYear(1992,11,3);
document.write(d);

</script>

</body>
</html>
```

Tue Nov 03 1992 23:05:36 GMT-0500 (Eastern Standard Time)

Figure 16.3

The following example demonstrates how to use toUTCString() to convert today's date (according to UTC) to a string.

Your results are shown in Figure 16.4.

```
<html>
<body>

<script type="text/javascript">

var d=new Date();
document.write("Original form: ");
document.write(d + "<br />");
document.write("To string (universal time): ");
document.write(d.toUTCString());

</script>

</body>
</html>
```

Original form: Wed Mar 10 2010 23:07:53 GMT-0500 (Eastern Standard Time)
To string (universal time): Thu, 11 Mar 2010 04:07:53 GMT

Figure 16.4

The getDay() method returns the day of the week as a number, with Sunday = 0. The following example demonstrates how to use getDay() and an array to display the day of the week as a text string rather than a number as shown in Figure 16.5.

```
<html>
<body>

<script type="text/javascript">

var d=new Date();
var weekday=new Array(7);
weekday[0]="Sunday";
weekday[1]="Monday";
weekday[2]="Tuesday";
```

```
weekday[3]="Wednesday";
weekday[4]="Thursday";
weekday[5]="Friday";
weekday[6]="Saturday";

document.write("Today is " + weekday[d.getDay()]);

</script>

</body>
</html>
```

```
Today is Wednesday
```

Figure 16.5

The following example demonstrates how to display a clock on your Web page.
Your results are shown in Figure 16.6.

Try it yourself >>

```
<html>
<head>
<script type="text/javascript">
function startTime()
{
var today=new Date();
var h=today.getHours();
var m=today.getMinutes();
var s=today.getSeconds();
// add a zero in front of numbers<10
m=checkTime(m);
s=checkTime(s);
document.getElementById('txt').innerHTML=h+":"+m+":"+s;
t=setTimeout('startTime()',500);
}

function checkTime(i)
{
if (i<10)
```

(continued)

93

(continued)

```
        {
        i="0" + i;
        }
    return i;
    }
</script>
</head>

<body onload="startTime()">
<div id="txt"></div>
</body>
</html>
```

```
23:13:51
```

Figure 16.6

CHAPTER 17

JAVASCRIPT ARRAY OBJECT

In This Chapter

❏ What Is an Array?

❏ Create an Array

❏ Access an Array

❏ Modify Values in an Array

❏ Examples

The Array object is used to store multiple values in a single variable.

What Is an Array?

An array is a special variable that can hold more than one value at a time.

If you have a list of items (a list of car names, for example), storing the cars in single variables could look like this:

```
cars1="Saab";
cars2="Volvo";
cars3="BMW";
```

However, what if you want to loop through the cars and find a specific one? And what if you had not three cars, but 300?

The best solution here is to use an array. An array can hold all your variable values under a single name. And you can access the values by referring to the array name.

Each element in the array has its own ID so that it can be easily accessed.

Create an Array

An array can be defined in three ways.

The following code creates an Array object called `myCars`:

1.

```
var myCars=new Array();
    // create a new array with no elements
    // new Array(n); will create a new array of length n
myCars[0]="Saab";
myCars[1]="Volvo";
myCars[2]="BMW";
```

2.

```
var myCars=new Array("Saab","Volvo","BMW");
// create a new array with the specified elements
```

3.

```
var myCars=["Saab","Volvo","BMW"];
//examples 2 & 3 are functionally equivalent
```

> **NOTE** If you specify numbers or true/false values inside the array then the variable type will be Number or Boolean, instead of String.

Access an Array

You can refer to a particular element in an array by referring to the name of the array and the index number. The index number starts at 0.

The following code line

```
document.write(myCars[0]);
```

results in the following output:

```
Saab
```

Modify Values in an Array

To modify a value in an existing array, just specify a new value for the element at the given index.

```
myCars[0]="Opel";  // overwrite the current value of
    myCars[0]
```

Now, the following code line:

```
document.write(myCars[0]);
```

results in the following output:

```
Opel
```

Examples

The following example demonstrates how to create an array, assign values to it, and write the values to the output.

Your results are shown in Figure 17.1.

Try it yourself >>

```
<html>
<body>

<script type="text/javascript">
var mycars = new Array();
mycars[0] = "Saab";
mycars[1] = "Volvo";
mycars[2] = "BMW";

for (i=0;i<mycars.length;i++)
{
document.write(mycars[i] + "<br />");
}
</script>

</body>
</html>
```

```
Saab
Volvo
BMW
```

Figure 17.1

The following example demonstrates how to use a `for...in` statement to loop through the elements of an array.

Your results are shown in Figure 17.2.

```
<html>
<body>
<script type="text/javascript">
var x;
var mycars = new Array();
mycars[0] = "Saab";
mycars[1] = "Volvo";
mycars[2] = "BMW";

for (x in mycars)
{
document.write(mycars[x] + "<br />");
}
</script>
</body>
</html>
```

```
Saab
Volvo
BMW
```

Figure 17.2

The following example demonstrates how to join two arrays. Your results are shown in Figure 17.3

```
<html>
<body>

<script type="text/javascript">

var parents = ["Jani", "Tove"];
var children = ["Cecilie", "Lone"];
var family = parents.concat(children);
document.write(family);
```

```
</script>

</body>
</html>
```

```
Jani,Tove,Cecilie,Lone
```

Figure 17.3

The following example demonstrates how to join three arrays. Your results are shown in Figure 17.4

```
<html>
<body>

<script type="text/javascript">

var parents = ["Jani", "Tove"];
var brothers = ["Stale", "Kai Jim", "Borge"];
var children = ["Cecilie", "Lone"];
var family = parents.concat(brothers, children);
document.write(family);

</script>

</body>
</html>
```

```
Jani,Tove,Stale,Kai Jim,Borge,Cecilie,Lone
```

Figure 17.4

The following example shows you how to join all elements of an array into a string. Your results are shown in Figure 17.5.

```
<html>
<body>

<script type="text/javascript">

var fruits = ["Banana", "Orange", "Apple", "Mango"];
document.write(fruits.join() + "<br />");
document.write(fruits.join("+") + "<br />");
```

(continued)

(continued)

```
      document.write(fruits.join(" and "));

</script>

</body>
</html>
```

```
Banana,Orange,Apple,Mango
Banana+Orange+Apple+Mango
Banana and Orange and Apple and Mango
```

Figure 17.5

The following example demonstrates how to remove the last element of an array, and Figure 17.6 shows your results.

```
<html>
<body>

<script type="text/javascript">

var fruits = ["Banana", "Orange", "Apple", "Mango"];
document.write(fruits.pop() + "<br />");
document.write(fruits + "<br />");
document.write(fruits.pop() + "<br />");
document.write(fruits);

</script>

</body>
</html>
```

```
Mango
Banana,Orange,Apple
Apple
Banana,Orange
```

Figure 17.6

The following example demonstrates how to add new elements to the end of an array. Your results are shown in Figure 17.7.

```
<html>
<body>
```

```
<script type="text/javascript">

var fruits = ["Banana", "Orange", "Apple", "Mango"];
document.write(fruits.push("Kiwi") + "<br />");
document.write(fruits.push("Lemon","Pineapple") + "<br />");
document.write(fruits);

</script>

</body>
</html>
```

```
5
7
Banana,Orange,Apple,Mango,Kiwi,Lemon,Pineapple
```

Figure 17.7

In the following example, you see how to reverse the order of the elements in an array. Your results are shown in Figure 17.8.

```
<html>
<body>

<script type="text/javascript">

var fruits = ["Banana", "Orange", "Apple", "Mango"];
document.write(fruits.reverse());

</script>

</body>
</html>
```

```
Mango,Apple,Orange,Banana
```

Figure 17.8

The following example demonstrates how to remove the first element of an array. Your results are shown in Figure 17.9.

```
<html>
<body>

<script type="text/javascript">
```

(continued)

(continued)

```
var fruits = ["Banana", "Orange", "Apple", "Mango"];
document.write(fruits.shift() + "<br />");
document.write(fruits + "<br />");
document.write(fruits.shift() + "<br />");
document.write(fruits);

</script>

</body>
</html>
```

```
Banana
Orange,Apple,Mango
Orange
Apple,Mango
```

Figure 17.9

The following example demonstrates how to use slice() to select elements from an array. Your results are shown in Figure 17.10.

```
<html>
<body>

<script type="text/javascript">

var fruits = ["Banana", "Orange", "Apple", "Mango"];
document.write(fruits.slice(0,1) + "<br />");
document.write(fruits.slice(1) + "<br />");
document.write(fruits.slice(-2) + "<br />");
document.write(fruits);

</script>

</body>
</html>
```

```
Banana
Orange,Apple,Mango
Apple,Mango
Banana,Orange,Apple,Mango
```

Figure 17.10

The following three examples demonstrate how to use **sort()**. The first **sort()** example shows how to sort alphabetically and ascending. Your results are shown in Figure 17.11.

```html
<html>
<body>

<script type="text/javascript">

var fruits = ["Banana", "Orange", "Apple", "Mango"];
document.write(fruits.sort());

</script>

</body>
</html>
```

```
Apple,Banana,Mango,Orange
```

Figure 17.11

The next **sort()** example demonstrates how to sort numerically and ascending. Your results are shown in Figure 17.12.

```html
<html>
<body>

<script type="text/javascript">

function sortNumber(a, b)
{
return a - b;
}

var n = ["10", "5", "40", "25", "100", "1"];
document.write(n.sort(sortNumber));

</script>

</body>
</html>
```

```
1,5,10,25,40,100
```

Figure 17.12

The third sort() example demonstrates how to sort numerically and descending. Your results are shown in Figure 17.13.

```
<html>
<body>

<script type="text/javascript">

function sortNumber(a, b)
{
return b - a;
}

var n = ["10", "5", "40", "25", "100", "1"];
document.write(n.sort(sortNumber));

</script>

</body>
</html>
```

```
100,40,25,10,5,1
```

Figure 17.13

The following example demonstrates how to use `splice()` to add an element to the second position in an array. Your results are shown in Figure 17.14.

```
<html>
<body>

<script type="text/javascript">

var fruits = ["Banana", "Orange", "Apple", "Mango"];
document.write("Removed: " + fruits.splice(2,0,"Lemon") +
   "<br />");
document.write(fruits);

</script>

</body>
</html>
```

```
Removed:
Banana,Orange,Lemon,Apple,Mango
```

Figure 17.14

The following example shows you how to convert an array to a string. Your results are shown in Figure 17.15.

```
<html>
<body>

<script type="text/javascript">

var fruits = ["Banana", "Orange", "Apple", "Mango"];
document.write(fruits.toString());

</script>

</body>
</html>
```

```
Banana,Orange,Apple,Mango
```

Figure 17.15

The following example shows you how to add new elements to the beginning of an array. Figure 17.16 shows your results.

```
<html>
<body>

<script type="text/javascript">

var fruits = ["Banana", "Orange", "Apple", "Mango"];
document.write(fruits.unshift("Kiwi") + "<br />");
document.write(fruits.unshift("Lemon","Pineapple") + "<br
   />");
document.write(fruits);

</script>

<p><b>Note:</b> The unshift() method does not work properly
   in Internet Explorer, it only returns undefined!</p>
```

(continued)

105

(continued)
```
      </body>
      </html>
```

```
5
7
Lemon,Pineapple,Kiwi,Banana,Orange,Apple,Mango
```

Figure 17.16

N O T E The unshift() method does not work properly in Internet Explorer, it only returns undefined, as shown in Figure 17.17.

```
undefined
undefined
Lemon,Pineapple,Kiwi,Banana,Orange,Apple,Mango
```

Figure 17.17

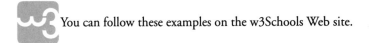 You can follow these examples on the w3Schools Web site.

For a complete reference of all the properties and methods that can be used with the Array object, go to the complete Array object reference in Appendix A.

CHAPTER 18

JAVASCRIPT BOOLEAN OBJECT

In This Chapter

❑ Create a Boolean Object

❑ Examples

The Boolean object is used to convert a non-Boolean value to a Boolean value (either true or false).

Create a Boolean Object

The Boolean object represents two values: true or false.

The following code creates a Boolean object called myBoolean:

```
var myBoolean=new Boolean();
```

> **NOTE** If the Boolean object has no initial value or if it is 0, -0, null, "", false, undefined, or NaN, the object is set to false. Otherwise, it is true (even with the string "false")!

All the following lines of code create Boolean objects with an initial value of false:

```
var myBoolean=new Boolean();
var myBoolean=new Boolean(0);
var myBoolean=new Boolean(null);
var myBoolean=new Boolean("");
var myBoolean=new Boolean(false);
var myBoolean=new Boolean(NaN);
```

And all the following lines of code create Boolean objects with an initial value of true:

```
var myBoolean=new Boolean(true);
var myBoolean=new Boolean("true");
var myBoolean=new Boolean("false");
var myBoolean=new Boolean("Richard");
```

For a complete reference of all the properties and methods that can be used with the Boolean object, go to the complete Boolean object reference in Appendix A.

Examples

The following example demonstrates how to check whether a Boolean object is true or false. Your result is shown in Figure 18.1.

Try it yourself >>

```
<html>
<body>

<script type="text/javascript">
var b1=new Boolean(0);
var b2=new Boolean(1);
var b3=new Boolean("");
var b4=new Boolean(null);
var b5=new Boolean(NaN);
var b6=new Boolean("false");

document.write("0 is boolean "+ b1 +"<br />");
document.write("1 is boolean "+ b2 +"<br />");
document.write("An empty string is boolean "+ b3 + "<br
    />");
document.write("null is boolean "+ b4+ "<br />");
document.write("NaN is boolean "+ b5 +"<br />");
document.write("The string 'false' is boolean "+ b6 +"<br
    />");
</script>

</body>
</html>
```

0 is boolean false
1 is boolean true
An empty string is boolean false
null is boolean false
NaN is boolean false
The string 'false' is boolean true

Figure 18.1

CHAPTER 19

JAVASCRIPT MATH OBJECT

In This Chapter

❑ Math Object

❑ Mathematical Constants

❑ Mathematical Methods

❑ Examples

The Math object allows you to perform mathematical tasks.

Math Object

The Math object allows you to perform mathematical tasks.

The Math object includes several mathematical constants and methods.

The syntax for using properties/methods of Math is as follows:

```
var pi_value=Math.PI;
var sqrt_value=Math.sqrt(16);
```

> **NOTE** The Math object is provided by JavaScript and does not need to be created by the programmer. In fact, trying to create a Math object using new() will result in a JavaScript error.

Mathematical Constants

JavaScript provides eight mathematical constants that can be accessed from the Math object. These are E, PI, square root of 2, square root of 1/2, natural log of 2, natural log of 10, base-2 log of E, and base-10 log of E.

You may reference these constants from your JavaScript like this:

```
Math.E
Math.PI
Math.SQRT2
Math.SQRT1_2
Math.LN2
Math.LN10
Math.LOG2E
Math.LOG10E
```

Mathematical Methods

In addition to the mathematical constants that can be accessed from the Math object, several methods also are available.

The following example uses the round() method of the Math object to round a number to the nearest integer:

```
document.write(Math.round(4.7));
```

The preceding code results in the following output:

```
5
```

The following example uses the random() method of the Math object to return a random number between 0 and 1:

```
document.write(Math.random());
```

The preceding code can result in the following output:

```
0.07730209357983464
```

The following example uses the floor() and random() methods of the Math object to return a random number between 0 and 10:

```
document.write(Math.floor(Math.random()*11));
```

The preceding code can result in the following output:

```
1
```

For a complete reference of all the properties and methods that can be used with the Math object, go to the complete Math object reference in Appendix A.

Examples

The following example demonstrates how to use round(). Your results are shown in Figure 19.1.

```
<html>
<body>

<script type="text/javascript">

document.write(Math.round(0.60) + "<br />");
document.write(Math.round(0.50) + "<br />");
document.write(Math.round(0.49) + "<br />");
document.write(Math.round(-4.40) + "<br />");
document.write(Math.round(-4.60));

</script>

</body>
</html>
```

```
1
1
0
-4
-5
```

Figure 19.1

The following example demonstrates how to use random() to return a random number between 0 and 1 as shown in Figure 19.2.

```
<html>
<body>

<script type="text/javascript">

//return a random number between 0 and 1
```

```
document.write(Math.random() + "<br />");

//return a random integer between 0 and 10
document.write(Math.floor(Math.random()*11));

</script>

</body>
</html>
```

```
0.42701333510622985
5
```

Figure 19.2

The following example demonstrates how to use max() to return the largest of the specified values. Your results are shown in Figure 19.3.

Try it yourself >>

```
<html>
<body>

<script type="text/javascript">

document.write(Math.max(5,10) + "<br />");
document.write(Math.max(0,150,30,20,38) + "<br />");
document.write(Math.max(-5,10) + "<br />");
document.write(Math.max(-5,-10) + "<br />");
document.write(Math.max(1.5,2.5));
</script>

</body>
</html>
```

```
10
150
10
-5
2.5
```

Figure 19.3

The following example shows how to use `min()` to return the smallest of the specified values. Your results are shown in Figure 19.4.

```
<html>
<body>

<script type="text/javascript">

document.write(Math.min(5,10) + "<br />");
document.write(Math.min(0,150,30,20,38) + "<br />");
document.write(Math.min(-5,10) + "<br />");
document.write(Math.min(-5,-10) + "<br />");
document.write(Math.min(1.5,2.5));

</script>

</body>
</html>
```

```
5
0
-5
-10
1.5
```

Figure 19.4

CHAPTER 20

JAVASCRIPT REGEXP OBJECT

In This Chapter

❑ What Is RegExp?

❑ RegExp Modifiers

❑ test()

❑ exec()

RegExp is short for regular expression.

What Is RegExp?

A regular expression is an object that describes a pattern of characters. When you search in a text, you can use a pattern to describe what you are searching for.

A simple pattern can be a single character. A more complicated pattern can consist of more characters and can be used for parsing, format checking, substitution, and more.

Regular expressions are used to perform powerful pattern-matching and search-and-replace functions on text.

The syntax is as follows:

```
var txt=new RegExp(pattern,modifiers);
```

or more simply:

```
var txt=/pattern/modifiers;
```

The syntax follows a couple of general guidelines:

▸▸ The pattern specifies the pattern of an expression.

▸▸ The modifiers specify whether a search should be global, case-sensitive, and so on.

RegExp Modifiers

Modifiers are used to perform case-insensitive and global searches.

The i modifier is used to perform case-insensitive matching.

The g modifier is used to perform a global match (find all matches rather than stopping after the first match).

The following example demonstrates how to do a case-insensitive search for "w3schools" in a string:

```
var str="Visit W3Schools";
var patt1=/w3schools/i;
```

Your results are shown in Figure 20.1.

Try it yourself >>

```
<html>
<body>

<script type="text/javascript">
var str = "Visit W3Schools";
var patt1 = /w3schools/i;
document.write(str.match(patt1));
</script>

</body>
</html>
```

W3Schools

Figure 20.1

The following example demonstrates how to do a global search for "is":

```
var str="Is this all there is?";
var patt1=/is/g;
```

Your results are shown in Figure 20.2.

Try it yourself >>

```
<html>
<body>

<script type="text/javascript">

var str="Is this all there is?";
var patt1=/is/g;
document.write(str.match(patt1));

</script>

</body>
</html>
```

```
is,is
```

Figure 20.2

The following example demonstrates how to do a global, case-insensitive search for "is":

```
var str="Is this all there is?";
var patt1=/is/gi;
```

Your results are shown in Figure 20.3.

Try it yourself >>

```
<html>
<body>
```

(continued)

(continued)

```
<script type="text/javascript">

var str="Is this all there is?";
var patt1=/is/gi;
document.write(str.match(patt1));

</script>

</body>
</html>
```

```
Is,is,is
```

Figure 20.3

test()

The test() method searches a string for a specified value and returns true or false, depending on the result.

The following example searches a string for the character "e":

```
var patt1=new RegExp("e");
document.write(patt1.test("The best things in life are
    free"));
```

Because there is an "e" in the string, the output of the preceding code is as follows:

```
true
```

Your results are shown in Figure 20.4.

Try it yourself >>

```
<html>
<body>

<script type="text/javascript">
var patt1=new RegExp("e");
```

```
document.write(patt1.test("The best things in life are
  free"));
</script>

</body>
</html>
```

```
true
```

Figure 20.4

exec()

The **exec()** method searches a string for a specified value and returns the text of the found value. If no match is found, it returns *null.*

The following example searches a string for the character "e":

```
var patt1=new RegExp("e");
document.write(patt1.exec("The best things in life are
  free"));
```

Because there is an "e" in the string, the output of the preceding code is:

```
e
```

Your results are shown in Figure 20.5.

| Try it yourself >> |

```
<html>
<body>

<script type="text/javascript">
var patt1=new RegExp("e");

document.write(patt1.exec("The best things in life are
  free"));
</script>

</body>
</html>
```

119

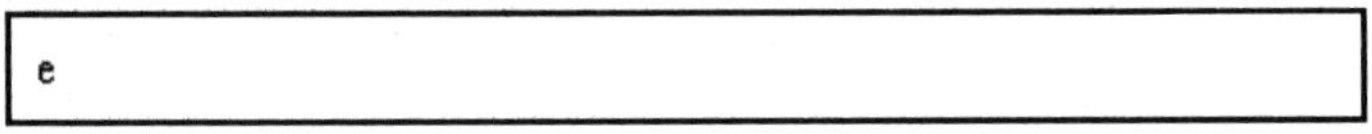

```
e
```

Figure 20.5

For a complete reference of all the properties and methods that can be used with the RegExp object, go to the complete RegExp object reference in Appendix A.

Section III
JavaScript
Advanced

CHAPTER 21

JAVASCRIPT BROWSER DETECTION

In This Chapter

❑ Browser Detection

❑ The Navigator Object

The Navigator object contains information about the visitor's browser.

Browser Detection

Almost everything in this tutorial works on all JavaScript-enabled browsers. However, some things just don't work on certain browsers—especially on older browsers.

So, sometimes it can be very useful to detect the visitor's browser and then serve up the appropriate information.

The best way to do this is to make your Web pages smart enough to look one way to some browsers and another way to other browsers. The Navigator object can be used for this purpose.

The Navigator object contains information about the visitor's browser name, version, and more.

> **NOTE** No public standard applies to the Navigator object, but all major browsers support it.

The Navigator Object

The Navigator object contains all information about the visitor's browser. We are going to look at two properties of the Navigator object:

▸▸ appName—holds the name of the browser

▸▸ appVersion—holds, among other things, the version of the browser

Your results are shown in Figure 21.1.

Try it yourself >>

```
<html>
<body>
<script type="text/javascript">
var browser=navigator.appName;
var b_version=navigator.appVersion;
var version=parseFloat(b_version);
document.write("Browser name: "+ browser);
document.write("<br />");
document.write("Browser version: "+ version);
</script>
</body>
</html>
```

```
Browser name: Netscape
Browser version: 5
```

Figure 21.1

The variable "browser" in the preceding example holds the name of the browser, that is, "Netscape" or "Microsoft Internet Explorer."

The appVersion property in the preceding example returns a string that contains much more information than just the version number, but for now we are only interested in the version number. To pull the version number out of the string, we are using a function called parseFloat(), which pulls the first thing that looks like a decimal number out of a string and returns it.

TIP To find the version number in IE 5.0 and later, you will have to dig a little deeper into either the appVersion or userAgent property. The IE version will be in the form "MSIE x.x" so use a regular expression such as /MSIE \d\.\d;/.exec(navigator.userAgent) to return a string containing the specific IE version.

The following example displays a different alert, depending on the visitor's browser. The alert box is shown in Figure 21.2.

```html
<html>
<head>
<script type="text/javascript">
function detectBrowser()
{
var browser=navigator.appName;
var b_version=navigator.appVersion;
var version=parseFloat(b_version);
if ((browser=="Netscape"||browser=="Microsoft Internet Ex-
  plorer") && (version>=4))
  {
  alert("Your browser is good enough!");
  }
else
  {
  alert("It's time to upgrade your browser!");
  }
}
</script>
</head>

<body onload="detectBrowser()">
</body>

</html>
```

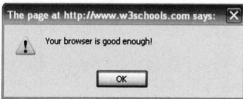

Figure 21.2

125

The following example provides more rules about the visitor's browser.
Your results are shown in Figure 21.3.

```
<html>
<body>
<script type="text/javascript">
document.write("<p>Browser: ");
document.write(navigator.appName + "</p>");

document.write("<p>Browserversion: ");
document.write(navigator.appVersion + "</p>");

document.write("<p>Code: ");
document.write(navigator.appCodeName + "</p>");

document.write("<p>Platform: ");
document.write(navigator.platform + "</p>");

document.write("<p>Cookies enabled: ");
document.write(navigator.cookieEnabled + "</p>");

document.write("<p>Browser's user agent header: ");
document.write(navigator.userAgent + "</p>");
</script>
</body>
</html>
```

Browser: Netscape

Browserversion: 5.0 (Windows; en-US)

Code: Mozilla

Platform: Win32

Cookies enabled: true

Browser's user agent header: Mozilla/5.0 (Windows; U; Windows NT 5.1;
en-US; rv:1.9.1.5) Gecko/20091102 Firefox/3.5.5 (.NET CLR 3.5.30729)

Figure 21.3

The following example provides ALL the details about the visitor's browser. Your results are shown in Figure 21.4.

```html
<html>
<body>

<script type="text/javascript">
var x = navigator;
document.write("CodeName=" + x.appCodeName);
document.write("<br />");
document.write("MinorVersion=" + x.appMinorVersion);
document.write("<br />");
document.write("Name=" + x.appName);
document.write("<br />");
document.write("Version=" + x.appVersion);
document.write("<br />");
document.write("CookieEnabled=" + x.cookieEnabled);
document.write("<br />");
document.write("CPUClass=" + x.cpuClass);
document.write("<br />");
document.write("OnLine=" + x.onLine);
document.write("<br />");
document.write("Platform=" + x.platform);
document.write("<br />");
document.write("UA=" + x.userAgent);
document.write("<br />");
document.write("BrowserLanguage=" + x.browserLanguage);
document.write("<br />");
document.write("SystemLanguage=" + x.systemLanguage);
document.write("<br />");
document.write("UserLanguage=" + x.userLanguage);
</script>

</body>
</html>
```

```
CodeName=Mozilla
MinorVersion=undefined
Name=Netscape
Version=5.0 (Windows; en-US)
CookieEnabled=true
CPUClass=undefined
OnLine=true
Platform=Win32
UA=Mozilla/5.0 (Windows; U; Windows NT 5.1; en-US; rv:1.9.1.5)
Gecko/20091102 Firefox/3.5.5 (.NET CLR 3.5.30729)
BrowserLanguage=undefined
SystemLanguage=undefined
UserLanguage=undefined
```

Figure 21.4

CHAPTER 22

JAVASCRIPT COOKIES

In This Chapter

❑ What Is a Cookie?

❑ Create and Store a Cookie

A cookie is often used to identify a user.

What Is a Cookie?

A cookie is a variable that is stored on the visitor's computer. Each time the same computer requests a page with a browser, it sends the cookie, too. With JavaScript, you can both create and retrieve cookie values.

Examples of cookies:

▸▸ **Name cookie.** The first time a visitor arrives on your Web page, she must fill in her name. The name then is stored in a cookie. Next time the visitor arrives at your page, she could get a welcome message like "Welcome Jane Doe!" The name is retrieved from the stored cookie.

▸▸ **Password cookie.** The first time a visitor arrives on your Web page, she must fill in a password. The password then is stored in a cookie. Next time the visitor arrives at your page, the password is retrieved from the cookie.

▸▸ **Date cookie.** The first time a visitor arrives to your Web page, the current date is stored in a cookie. Next time the visitor arrives at your page, she could get a message like "Your last visit was on Tuesday, August 11, 2005!" The date is retrieved from the stored cookie.

Create and Store a Cookie

In this example we create a cookie that stores the name of a visitor. The first time a visitor arrives at the Web page, she is asked to fill in her name. The name then is stored in a cookie. The next time the visitor arrives at the same page, she sees a welcome message.

First, we create a function that stores the name of the visitor in a cookie variable:

```
function setCookie(c_name,value,expiredays)
{
var exdate=new Date();
exdate.setDate(exdate.getDate()+expiredays);
document.cookie=c_name+ "=" +escape(value)+
((expiredays==null) ? "" : ";expires="+exdate.toGMTString());
}
```

The parameters of the preceding function hold the name of the cookie, the value of the cookie, and the number of days until the cookie expires.

In the preceding function, we first convert the number of days to a valid date and then we add the number of days until the cookie should expire. After that, we store the cookie name, cookie value, and the expiration date in the **document.cookie** object.

Then we create another function that checks whether the cookie has been set:

```
function getCookie(c_name)
{
if (document.cookie.length>0)
  {
  c_start=document.cookie.indexOf(c_name + "=");
  if (c_start!=-1)
    {
    c_start=c_start + c_name.length+1;
    c_end=document.cookie.indexOf(";",c_start);
    if (c_end==-1) c_end=document.cookie.length;
    return unescape(document.cookie.substring(c_start,c_
  end));
    }
  }
return "";
}
```

The preceding function first checks whether a cookie is stored at all in the document.cookie object. If the document.cookie object holds some cookies, then check to see whether our specific cookie is stored. If our cookie is found, then return the value; if not, return an empty string.

Last, we create the function that displays a welcome message if the cookie is set, and if the cookie is not set, it displays a prompt box asking for the name of the user:

```
function checkCookie()
{
username=getCookie('username');
if (username!=null && username!="")
  {
  alert('Welcome again '+username+'!');
  }
else
  {
  username=prompt('Please enter your name:',"");
  if (username!=null && username!="")
    {
    setCookie('username',username,365);
    }
  }
}
```

The following example runs the checkCookie() function when the page loads. The resulting dialog box is shown in Figure 22.1.

Try it yourself >>

```
<html>
<head>
<script type="text/javascript">
function getCookie(c_name)
{
if (document.cookie.length>0)
  {
  c_start=document.cookie.indexOf(c_name + "=");
  if (c_start!=-1)
    {
    c_start=c_start + c_name.length+1 ;
    c_end=document.cookie.indexOf(";",c_start);
    if (c_end==-1) c_end=document.cookie.length
```

(continued)

131

(continued)

```
      return unescape(document.cookie.substring(c_start,c_
    end));
      }
   }
return ""
}

function setCookie(c_name,value,expiredays)
{
var exdate=new Date();
exdate.setDate(exdate.getDate()+expiredays);
document.cookie=c_name+ "=" +escape(value)+((expiredays=
  =null) ? "" : "; expires="+exdate.toGMTString());
}

function checkCookie()
{
username=getCookie('username');
if (username!=null && username!="")
  {
  alert('Welcome again '+username+'!');
  }
else
  {
  username=prompt('Please enter your name:',"");
  if (username!=null && username!="")
    {
    setCookie('username',username,365);
    }
  }
}
</script>
</head>
<body onLoad="checkCookie()">
</body>
</html>
```

Explorer User Prompt
Script Prompt:
Please enter your name:
OK
Cancel

Figure 22.1

CHAPTER 23

JAVASCRIPT FORM VALIDATION

In This Chapter

❏ Required Fields

❏ E-mail Validation

JavaScript can be used to validate data in HTML forms before sending off the content to a server.

Form data that typically are checked by a JavaScript could be:

▸▸ Has the user left required fields empty?

▸▸ Has the user entered a valid e-mail address?

▸▸ Has the user entered a valid date?

▸▸ Has the user entered text in a numeric field?

Required Fields

The following function checks whether a required field has been left empty. If the required field is blank, an alert is displayed, and the function returns false. If a value is entered, the function returns true (means that data is OK):

```
function validate_required(field,alerttxt)
{
with (field)
  {
  if (value==null||value=="")
    {
    alert(alerttxt);return false;
    }
  else
```

```
      {
      return true;
      }
   }
}
```

The entire script with the HTML form could look something like this:

```
<html>
<head>
<script type="text/javascript">
function validate_required(field,alerttxt)

{
with (field)
  {
  if (value==null||value=="")
    {
    alert(alerttxt);return false;
    }
  else
    {
    return true;
    }
  }
}

function validate_form(thisform)
{
with (thisform)
  {
  if (validate_required(email,"Email must be filled
  out!")==false)
  {email.focus();return false;}
  }
}
</script>
</head>

<body>
```

(continued)

(continued)

```
<form action="submit.htm" onsubmit="return validate_
   form(this)" method="post">
Email: <input type="text" name="email" size="30">
<input type="submit" value="Submit">
</form>
</body>

</html>
```

E-mail Validation

The following function checks whether the content follows the general syntax of an e-mail address.

> **N O T E** This function only checks that the content appears to be an e-mail with the proper format. It does not verify that the e-mail address actually exists.

This means that the input data must contain at least an @ sign and a dot (.). Also, the @ must not be the first character of the e-mail address, and the last dot must at least be one character after the @ sign:

```
function validate_email(field,alerttxt)
{
with (field)
  {
  apos=value.indexOf("@");
  dotpos=value.lastIndexOf(".");
  if (apos<1||dotpos-apos<2)
    {alert(alerttxt);return false;}
  else {return true;}
  }
}
```

The entire script with the HTML form could look something like this:

```
<html>
<head>
<script type="text/javascript">
function validate_email(field,alerttxt)
{
```

```
with (field)
  {
  apos=value.indexOf("@");
  dotpos=value.lastIndexOf(".");
  if (apos<1||dotpos-apos<2)
    {alert(alerttxt);return false;}
  else {return true;}
  }
}

function validate_form(thisform)
{
with (thisform)
  {
  if (validate_email(email,"Not a valid e-mail
  address!")==false)
    {email.focus();return false;}
  }
}
</script>
</head>

<body>
<form action="submit.htm" onsubmit="return validate_
  form(this);" method=get>
Email: <input type="text" name="email" size="30">
<input type="submit" value="Submit">
</form>
</body>

</html>
```

CHAPTER 24

JAVASCRIPT ANIMATION

In This Chapter

- ❑ The HTML Code
- ❑ The JavaScript Code
- ❑ The Entire Code

With JavaScript, we can create animated images.

The trick is to let a JavaScript change between different images on different events.

In the following example, we add an image that should act as a link button on a Web page. We then add an `onMouseOver` event and an `onMouseOut` event that will run two JavaScript functions that change between the images.

The HTML Code

The HTML code looks like this:

```
<a href="http://www.w3schools.com" target="_blank">
<img border="0" alt="Visit w3schools!" src="b_pink.gif"
    id="b1"
onmouseOver="mouseOver()" onmouseOut="mouseOut()" /></a>
```

Note that we have given the image an `id`, to make it possible for JavaScript to address it later.

The `onMouseOver` event tells the browser that once a mouse is rolled over the image, the browser should execute a function that replaces the image with another image.

The `onMouseOut` event tells the browser that once a mouse is rolled away from the image, another JavaScript function should be executed. This function inserts the original image again.

The JavaScript Code

The changing between the images is done with the following JavaScript:

```
<script type="text/javascript">
function mouseOver()
{
document.getElementById("b1").src ="b_blue.gif";
}
function mouseOut()
{
document.getElementById("b1").src ="b_pink.gif";
}
</script>
```

The function mouseOver() causes the image to shift to "b_blue.gif."

The function mouseOut() causes the image to shift to "b_pink.gif."

The Entire Code

In the following example, we combine the HTML and JavaScript code to produce animation.

The resulting animation is shown in Figure 24.1.

You can try this example on the www.w3schools.com Web site or include you own graphic files in the directory with your html source, substituting for b_blue and b_pink in the html source code.

Try it yourself >>

```
<html>
<head>
<script type="text/javascript">
function mouseOver()
{
document.getElementById("b1").src ="b_blue.gif";
}
function mouseOut()
{
document.getElementById("b1").src ="b_pink.gif";
}
```

(continued)

(continued)

```
    </script>
    </head>

    <body>
    <a href="http://www.w3schools.com" target="_blank">
    <img border="0" alt="Visit w3schools!" src="b_pink.gif"
      id="b1"
    width="26" height="26" onmouseover="mouseOver()"
      onmouseout="mouseOut()" /></a>
    </body>
    </html>
```

Figure 24.1

CHAPTER 25

JAVASCRIPT IMAGE MAPS

In This Chapter

❑ HTML Image Maps

❑ Adding Some JavaScript

An image map is an image with clickable regions.

HTML Image Maps

 If you've read *Learn HTML and CSS with w3schools* or completed the HTML tutorial on the w3schools Web site, you know that an image map is an image with clickable regions. Normally, each region has an associated hyperlink. Clicking on one of the regions takes you to the associated link. Look at the simple HTML image map.

The result of an image map is shown in Figure 25.1.

Try it yourself >>

```
<html>

<body>
<img src ="planets.gif" width ="145" height ="126"
  alt="Planets" usemap="#planetmap" />

<map name="planetmap">
<area shape ="rect" coords ="0,0,82,126"
href ="sun.htm" target ="_blank" alt="Sun" />

<area shape ="circle" coords ="90,58,3"
```

(continued)

141

(continued)

```
        href ="mercur.htm" target ="_blank" alt="Mercury" />

        <area shape ="circle" coords ="124,58,8"
        href ="venus.htm" target ="_blank" alt="Venus" />
        </map>

        </body>
        </html>
```

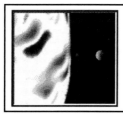

Figure 25.1

Adding Some JavaScript

We can add events (that can call a JavaScript) to the <area> tags inside the image map. The <area> tag supports the onClick, onDblClick, onMouseDown, onMouseUp, onMouseOver, onMouseMove, onMouseOut, onKeyPress, onKey-Down, onKeyUp, onFocus, and onBlur events.

Here's the HTML image-map example, with some JavaScript added. Your results are shown in Figure 25.2.

Try it yourself >>

```
<html>
<head>
<script type="text/javascript">
function writeText(txt)
{
document.getElementById("desc").innerHTML=txt;
}
</script>
</head>

<body>
```

```
<img src ="planets.gif" width ="145" height ="126"
  alt="Planets"
usemap="#planetmap" />


<map name="planetmap">
<area shape ="rect" coords ="0,0,82,126"
onMouseOver="writeText('The Sun and the gas giant planets
  like Jupiter are by far the largest objects in our Solar
  System.')"
href ="sun.htm" target ="_blank" alt="Sun" />


<area shape ="circle" coords ="90,58,3"
onMouseOver="writeText('The planet Mercury is very difficult
  to study from the Earth because it is always so close to
  the Sun.')"
href ="mercur.htm" target ="_blank" alt="Mercury" />


<area shape ="circle" coords ="124,58,8"
onMouseOver="writeText('Until the 1960s, Venus was often
  considered a  twin sister to the Earth because Venus is
  the nearest planet to us, and because the two planets seem
  to share many characteristics.')"
href ="venus.htm" target ="_blank" alt="Venus" />
</map>


<p id="desc"></p>


</body>
</html>
```

Figure 25.2

CHAPTER 26

JAVASCRIPT TIMING EVENTS

In This Chapter

❑ The setTimeout() Method

❑ The clearTimeout() Method

With JavaScript, it is possible to execute some code after a specified time interval. This is called timing events.

It's very easy to time events in JavaScript. The two key methods that are used are as follows:

▸▸ setTimeout()–Executes a code some time in the future

▸▸ clearTimeout()–Cancels the setTimeout()

> **NOTE** The setTimeout() and clearTimeout() are both methods of the HTML DOM Window object.

The setTimeout() Method

The syntax is as follows:

```
var t=setTimeout("javascript statement",milliseconds);
```

The setTimeout() method returns a value. In the preceding statement, the value is stored in a variable called *t*. If you want to cancel this setTimeout(), you can refer to it using the variable name.

The first parameter of setTimeout() is a string that contains a JavaScript statement. This statement could be a statement like "alert('5 seconds!')" or a call to a function, like "alertMsg()".

The second parameter indicates how many milliseconds from now you want to execute the first parameter.

> **N O T E** There are 1000 milliseconds in 1 second.

When the button is clicked in the following example, an alert box is displayed after 3 seconds.

Your results are shown in Figure 26.1.

Try it yourself >>

```
<html>
<head>
<script type="text/javascript">
function timedMsg()
{
var t=setTimeout("alert('I am displayed after 3
   seconds!')",3000);
}
</script>
</head>

<body>
<form>
<input type="button" value="Display alert box!"
   onClick="timedMsg()" />
</form>
</body>

</html>
```

| Display alert box! |

Figure 26.1

To get a timer to work in an infinite loop, you must write a function that calls itself.

In the following example, when a button is clicked, the input field starts to count (forever) starting at 0.

Notice that you also have a function that checks whether the timer is already running, to avoid creating additional timers if the button is clicked more than once.

Your results are shown in Figure 26.2.

```html
<html>
<head>
<script type="text/javascript">
var c=0;
var t;
var timer_is_on=0;

function timedCount()
{
document.getElementById('txt').value=c;
c=c+1;
t=setTimeout("timedCount()",1000);
}

function doTimer()
{
if (!timer_is_on)
  {
  timer_is_on=1;
  timedCount();
  }
}
</script>
</head>

<body>
<form>
<input type="button" value="Start count!"
  onClick="doTimer()">
<input type="text" id="txt">
</form>
<p>Click on the button above. The input field will count for-
  ever, starting at 0.</p>
</body>
</html>
```

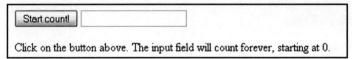

Start count! _____

Click on the button above. The input field will count forever, starting at 0.

Figure 26.2

The following example is another simple timing using the setTimeout() method. Your results are shown in Figure 26.3.

```html
<html>
<head>
<script type="text/javascript">
function timedText()
{
var t1=setTimeout("document.getElementById('txt').value='2
  seconds!'",2000);
var t2=setTimeout("document.getElementById('txt').value='4
  seconds!'",4000);
var t3=setTimeout("document.getElementById('txt').value='6
  seconds!'",6000);
}
</script>
</head>

<body>
<form>
<input type="button" value="Display timed text!"
  onclick="timedText()" />
<input type="text" id="txt" />
</form>
<p>Click on the button above. The input field will tell you
  when two, four, and six seconds have passed.</p>
</body>

</html>
```

Display timed text!	

Click on the button above. The input field will tell you when two, four, and six seconds have passed.

Figure 26.3

The following example shows a clock created with a timing event.

Your results are shown in Figure 26.4.

Try it yourself >>

```
<html>
<head>
<script type="text/javascript">
function startTime()
{
var today=new Date();
var h=today.getHours();
var m=today.getMinutes();
var s=today.getSeconds();
// add a zero in front of numbers<10
m=checkTime(m);
s=checkTime(s);
document.getElementById('txt').innerHTML=h+":"+m+":"+s;
t=setTimeout('startTime()',500);
}

function checkTime(i)
{
if (i<10)
  {
  i="0" + i;
  }
return i;
}
</script>
</head>
```

```
<body onload="startTime()">
<div id="txt"></div>
</body>
</html>
```

```
21:34:38
```

Figure 26.4

The clearTimeout() Method

The syntax is as follows:

```
clearTimeout(setTimeout_variable)
```

The following example is the same as the previous infinite loop example. The only difference is that we have now added a `"Stop Count!"` button that stops the timer. Your results are shown in Figure 26.5.

Try it yourself >>

```
<html>
<head>
<script type="text/javascript">
var c=0;
var t;
var timer_is_on=0;

function timedCount()
{
document.getElementById('txt').value=c;
c=c+1;
t=setTimeout("timedCount()",1000);
}

function doTimer()
{
```

(continued)

(continued)

```
    if (!timer_is_on)
      {
      timer_is_on=1;
      timedCount();
      }
    }

    function stopCount()
    {
    clearTimeout(t);
    timer_is_on=0;
    }
    </script>
    </head>

    <body>
    <form>
    <input type="button" value="Start count!" onclick="doTimer()"
      />
    <input type="text" id="txt" />
    <input type="button" value="Stop count!"
      onclick="stopCount()" />
    </form>
    <p>
    Click on the "Start count!" button above to start the timer.
      The input field will count forever, starting at 0. Click on
      the "Stop count!" button to stop the counting. Click on
      the "Start count!" button to start the timer again.
    </p>
    </body>
    </html>
```

Start count! | | Stop count!

Click on the "Start count!" button above to start the timer. The input field will count forever, starting at 0. Click on the "Stop count!" button to stop the counting. Click on the "Start count!" button to start the timer again.

Figure 26.5

CHAPTER 27

CREATE YOUR OWN OBJECTS WITH JAVASCRIPT

In This Chapter

❏ JavaScript Objects

❏ Creating Your Own Objects

Objects are useful to organize information.

JavaScript Objects

Earlier in this book, you learned that JavaScript has several built-in objects, like String, Date, Array, and more. In addition to these built-in objects, you also can create your own.

An object is just a special kind of data, a collection of properties and methods.

Let's illustrate with an example and create an object that models a person. Properties are the values associated with the object. The person's properties include name, height, weight, age, skin tone, eye color, and so on. All persons have these properties, but the values of those properties differ from person to person. Objects also have methods. Methods are the actions that can be performed on objects. The person's methods could be eat(), sleep(), work(), play(), and so on.

Properties

The syntax for accessing a property of an object is as follows:

```
objName.propName
```

You can add a property to an object by simply giving it a value. Assume that the `personObj` already exists; you can give it properties named `firstname`, `lastname`, `age`, and `eyecolor` as follows:

```
personObj.firstname="John";
personObj.lastname="Doe";
personObj.age=30;
personObj.eyecolor="blue";

document.write(personObj.firstname);
```

The preceding code generates the following output:

```
John
```

Methods

An object also can contain methods.

You can call a method with the following syntax:

```
objName.methodName()
```

> **NOTE** Parameters required for the method can be passed between the parentheses.

To call a method called `sleep()` for the `personObj`:

```
personObj.sleep();
```

If the `sleep()` method accepts a parameter for the number of hours, it could be called like this:

```
personObj.sleep(8)
```

Creating Your Own Objects

There are two ways to create a new object: You can create a direct instance of an object, or you can create a template of an object.

Create a Direct Instance of an Object

The following code creates an instance of an object and adds four properties to it:

```
personObj=new Object();
personObj.firstname="John";
```

```
personObj.lastname="Doe";
personObj.age=50;
personObj.eyecolor="blue";
```

Adding a method to the `personObj` is also simple. The following code adds a method called `eat()` to the `personObj`:

```
personObj.eat=eat;
```

In the following example, you create a direct instance of an object.

Your results are shown in Figure 27.1.

Try it yourself >>

```
<html>
<body>

<script type="text/javascript">
personObj=new Object();
personObj.firstname="John";
personObj.lastname="Doe";
personObj.age=50;
personObj.eyecolor="blue";

document.write(personObj.firstname + " is " + personObj.age +
    " years old.");
</script>

</body>
</html>
```

```
John is 50 years old.
```

Figure 27.1

Create a Template of an Object

The template defines the structure of an object so that you can more easily create multiple instances of that object:

```
function person(firstname,lastname,age,eyecolor)
{
this.firstname=firstname;
this.lastname=lastname;
this.age=age;
this.eyecolor=eyecolor;
}
```

Notice that the template is just a function.

It is also called a **constructor**. Inside the constructor, you add the properties and methods that will belong to each subsequent instance of the object. When you use *person* as a constructor for more than one object, you must include the "this" keyword. JavaScript uses "this" to assign the properties to the specific object created with the "new" keyword.

In the following example, you create a template for an object.

Your results are shown in Figure 27.2.

Try it yourself >>

```
<html>
<body>

<script type="text/javascript">
function person(firstname,lastname,age,eyecolor)
{
this.firstname=firstname;
this.lastname=lastname;
this.age=age;
this.eyecolor=eyecolor;
}

myFather=new person("John","Doe",50,"blue");

document.write(myFather.firstname + " is " + myFather.age + "
    years old.");
</script>
```

```
</body>
</html>
```

John is 50 years old.

Figure 27.2

After you have the template, you can create new instances of the object, like this:

```
myFather=new person("John","Doe",50,"blue"); myMother=new
   person("Sally","Rally",48,"green");
```

You can also add some methods to the person object. This is also done inside the template:

```
function person(firstname,lastname,age,eyecolor)
{
this.firstname=firstname;
this.lastname=lastname;
this.age=age;
this.eyecolor=eyecolor;

this.newlastname=newlastname;
}
```

Note that methods are just functions attached to objects. Then you will have to write the newlastname() function:

```
function newlastname(new_lastname)
{
this.lastname=new_lastname;
}
```

The newlastname() function defines the person's new last name and assigns that to the person. JavaScript knows which person you're talking about by using "this." So, now you can write: myMother.newlastname("Doe").

Section IV
AJAX Basic

CHAPTER 28

AJAX XMLHTTPREQUEST

In This Chapter

AJAX Uses the XMLHttpRequest Object

To get or send information from/to a database or a file on the server with traditional JavaScript, you will have to make an HTML form. A user will have to click the Submit button to send/get the information and wait for the server to respond. Then a new page will load with the results. Because the server returns a new page each time the user submits input, traditional Web applications can run slowly and tend to be less user friendly.

With AJAX, your JavaScript communicates directly with the server through the JavaScript XMLHttpRequest object.

With the XMLHttpRequest object, a Web page can make a request to, and get a response from a Web server—without reloading the page. The user will stay on the same page, and he will not notice that scripts request pages or send data to a server in the background.

The XMLHttpRequest Object

By using the XMLHttpRequest object, a Web developer can update a page with data from the server after the page has loaded!

AJAX was made popular in 2005 by Google (with Google Suggest).

Google Suggest is using the XMLHttpRequest object to create a very dynamic Web interface: When you start typing in Google's search box, a JavaScript sends the letters off to a server, and the server returns a list of suggestions.

The XMLHttpRequest object is supported in all major browsers (Internet Explorer, Firefox, Chrome, Opera, and Safari).

Your First AJAX Application

To understand how AJAX works, we will create a small AJAX application.

We will create an AJAX application from scratch. The application will use two click buttons to fetch data from a server and display the information in a Web page without reloading the page itself.

First, create a small HTML page with a short <div> section. The <div> section will be used to display alternative information requested from a server.

To identify the <div> section, we use an id="test" attribute:

```
<html>
<body>

<div id="test">
<h2>Clickto let AJAX change this text</h2>
</div>

<body>
</html>
```

Then we add two simple <buttons>. When they are clicked the buttons will call a function loadXMLDoc():

```
<button type="button" onclick="loadXMLDoc('test1.txt')">Click
    Me</button>
<button type="button" onclick="loadXMLDoc('test2.txt')">Click
    Me</button>
```

Finally, we add a <script> to the page's <head> section to contain the loadXML Doc() function:

```
<head>
<script type="text/javascript">
function loadXMLDoc(url)
{
```

```
.... Your AJAX script goes here ...
}
</script>
</head>
```

The next chapters explain the script (using AJAX) and how to make the application work.

 The various supporting files and images, including the test1.txt and test2.txt files, are accessed when completing this tutorial online at www. w3schools.com.

Your results are shown in Figure 28.1.

Try it yourself >>

```
<html>
<head>
<script type="text/javascript">
function loadXMLDoc(url)
{
if (window.XMLHttpRequest)
  {// code for IE7+, Firefox, Chrome, Opera, Safari
  xmlhttp=new XMLHttpRequest();
  }
else
  {// code for IE6, IE5
  xmlhttp=new ActiveXObject("Microsoft.XMLHTTP");
  }
xmlhttp.open("GET",url,false);
xmlhttp.send(null);
document.getElementById('test').innerHTML=xmlhttp.response-
  Text;
}
</script>
</head>

<body>

<div id="test">
<h2>Clickto let AJAX change this text</h2>
```

(continued)

161

(continued)

```
        </div>
        <button type="button" onclick="loadXMLDoc('test1.txt')">Click
          Me</button>

        <button type="button" onclick="loadXMLDoc('test2.txt')">Click
          Me</button>

        </body>
        </html>
```

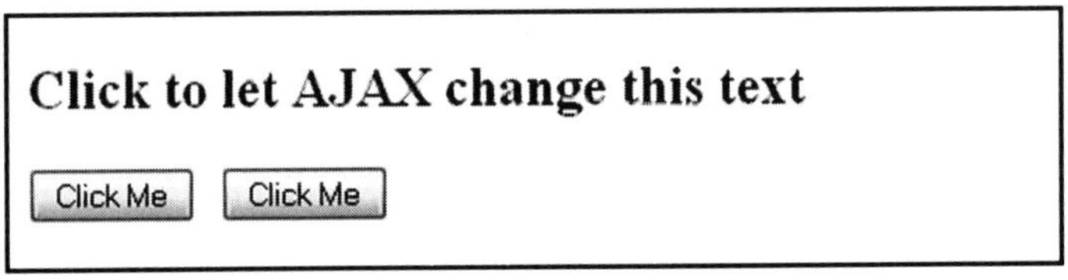

Click to let AJAX change this text

[Click Me]   [Click Me]

Figure 28.1

CHAPTER 29

AJAX BROWSER SUPPORT

In This Chapter

❑ The XMLHttpRequest

❑ All Together Now

The keystone of AJAX is the XMLHttpRequest object.

The XMLHttpRequest

All new browsers support a new built-in JavaScript XMLHttpRequest object (IE5 and IE6 use an ActiveXObject).

The XMLHttpRequest object can be used to request information (data) from a server.

Let's update our HTML file with a JavaScript in the <head> section:

```
function loadXMLDoc(url)
{
if (window.XMLHttpRequest)
{// code for IE7+, Firefox, Chrome, Opera, Safari
xmlhttp=new XMLHttpRequest();
}
else
{// code for IE6, IE5
xmlhttp=new ActiveXObject("Microsoft.XMLHTTP");
}
xmlhttp.open("GET",url,false);
xmlhttp.send(null);
document.getElementById('test').innerHTML=xmlhttp.response-
  Text;
}
```

Try to create an `XMLHttpRequest` object:

```
xmlhttp=new XMLHttpRequest()
```

If not (if IE5 or IE6), create an `ActiveXObject`:

```
xmlhttp=new ActiveXObject("Microsoft.XMLHTTP")
```

Open the request object:

```
xmlhttp.open("GET",url,false)
```

Send your request to your server:

```
xmlhttp.send(null)
```

Update your page with the response from the server:

```
document.getElementById('test').innerHTML=xmlhttp.response-
   Text
```

> **NOTE** The preceding code can be used every time you need to create an XML `HttpRequest` object, so just copy and paste it whenever you need it.

In Chapter 30, "AJAX—the XMLHttpRequest Object", you learn more about the `XMLHttpRequest`.

All Together Now

The following example puts what you've learned all together.

Your results are shown in Figure 29.1.

Try it yourself >>

```
<html>
<head>
<script type="text/javascript">
function loadXMLDoc(url)
{
if (window.XMLHttpRequest)
  {// code for IE7+, Firefox, Chrome, Opera, Safari
  xmlhttp=new XMLHttpRequest();
```

```
    }
else
    {// code for IE6, IE5
    xmlhttp=new ActiveXObject("Microsoft.XMLHTTP");
    }
xmlhttp.open("GET",url,false);
xmlhttp.send(null);
document.getElementById('test').innerHTML=xmlhttp.response-
    Text;
}
</script>
</head>

<body>

<div id="test">
<h2>Click to let AJAX change this text</h2>
</div>
<button type="button" onclick="loadXMLDoc('test1.txt')">Click
    Me</button>

<button type="button" onclick="loadXMLDoc('test2.txt')">Click
    Me</button>

</body>
</html>
```

Figure 29.1

CHAPTER 30

AJAX—THE XMLHTTPREQUEST OBJECT'S METHODS AND PROPERTIES

In This Chapter

- ❏ Important Methods
- ❏ Sending an AJAX Request to a Server
- ❏ Important Properties
- ❏ The responseText Property
- ❏ XMLHttpRequest Open—Using False
- ❏ XMLHttpRequest Open—Using True
- ❏ The readyState Property
- ❏ The onreadystatechange Property

In this chapter, you learn about important **methods** and **properties** of the XMLHttpRequest object.

Important Methods

The XMLHttpRequest object has two important methods:

▶ The open() method
▶ The send() method

Sending an AJAX Request to a Server

To send a request to a Web server, use the open() and send() methods.

The open() method takes three arguments. The first argument defines which method to use (GET or POST). The second argument specifies the name of the server resource (URL). The third argument specifies if the request should be handled asynchronously.

The send() method sends the request off to the server. If we assume the file requested is called time.asp, the code would be:

```
url="time.asp"
xmlhttp.open("GET",url,true);
xmlhttp.send(null);
```

In the example, we assume that the current Web page and the requested resource are both in the same file directory.

Important Properties

The XMLHttpRequest object has three important properties:

▶▶ The responseText property

▶▶ The readyState property

▶▶ The onreadystatechange property

The responseText Property

The XMLHttpRequest object stores any data retrieved from a server as a result of a server request in its responseText property.

In the previous chapter, you copied the content of the responseText property into your HTML with the following statement:

```
document.getElementById('test').innerHTML=xmlhttp.response-
   Text
```

XMLHttpRequest Open—Using False

In the previous examples, we used this simplified syntax:

```
xmlhttp.open("GET",url,false);
xmlhttp.send(null);
document.getElementById('test').innerHTML=xmlhttp.
   responseText;
```

167

The third parameter in the open call is "false". This tells the XMLHttpRequest object to wait until the server request is completed before next statement is executed.

For small applications and simple server requests, this might be OK. But if the request takes a long time or cannot be served, this might cause your Web application to hang or stop.

XMLHttpRequest Open—Using True

By changing the third parameter in the open call to "true", you tell the XMLHttpRequest object to continue the execution after the request to the server has been sent.

Because you cannot simply start using the response from the server request before you are sure the request has been completed, you need to set the onreadystatechange property of the XMLHttpRequest, to a function (or name of a function) to be executed after completion.

In this onreadystatechange function, you must test the readyState property before you can use the result of the server call.

Simply change the code to

```
xmlhttp.onreadystatechange=function()
{
if(xmlhttp.readyState==4)  HB: // request is complete
  {document.getElementById('test').innerHTML=xmlhttp.
  responseText}
}
xmlhttp.open("GET",url,true);
xmlhttp.send(null);
```

The readyState Property

The readyState property holds the status of the server's response.

Possible values for the readyState property are shown in the following table.

State	Description
0	The request is not initialized
1	The request has been set up
2	The request has been sent
3	The request is in process
4	The request is complete

The onreadystatechange Property

The onreadystatechange property stores a function (or the name of a function) to be called automatically each time the readyState property changes.

You can define the entire function in the property like this:

```
xmlhttp.onreadystatechange=function()
{
if(xmlhttp.readyState==4)
  {document.getElementById('test').innerHTML=xmlhttp.
  responseText}
}
xmlhttp.open("GET",url,true);
xmlhttp.send(null);
```

Or you can simply store the name of a function that is defined elsewhere, like this:

```
xmlhttp.onreadystatechange=state_Change
xmlhttp.open("GET",url,true);
xmlhttp.send(null);
...
...
...
function state_Change()
{
if(xmlhttp.readyState==4)
  {document.getElementById('test').innerHTML=xmlhttp.
  responseText}
}
```

CHAPTER 31

AJAX SERVER

In This Chapter

❑ XMLHttpRequest Object Can Request Any Data

❑ Requesting Files

❑ Submitting Forms

There is no such thing as an AJAX server.

XMLHttpRequest Object Can Request Any Data

With the XMLHttpRequest object, you can request any Web resource from a server.

You can request TXT files, HTML files, XML files, pictures, or any data that is accessible from the Internet.

> **NOTE** AJAX is about creating clever applications that can use the data.

Requesting Files

Many AJAX applications request pure text files to retrieve data for the application.

A very common AJAX method is to request XML files to retrieve application data.

Requesting an ASP or PHP file is the most common way to access database information.

Requesting HTML files is a common method for filling out different information on a Web page.

Submitting Forms

With AJAX, you can easily submit form data without having to reload the page.

In the following chapters, we request data and files and learn how to submit forms.

Section V
AJAX Advanced

❑ **Chapter 32: AJAX Suggest**

❑ **Chapter 33: AJAX Database Example**

❑ **Chapter 34: AJAX XML Example**

❑ **Chapter 35: AJAX ResponseXML Example**

AJAX SUGGEST

In This Chapter

- ❑ The HTML Form
- ❑ The showHint() Function
- ❑ The GetXmlHttpObject() Function
- ❑ The stateChanged() Function
- ❑ AJAX Suggest Source Code

AJAX can be used to create more interactive applications.

The following AJAX example demonstrates how a Web page can communicate with a Web server while a user enters data into an HTML form.

For this example, use the name "Kelly." Note what happens as you type a name in the input field, as shown in Figure 32.1.

Figure 32.1

The HTML Form

The preceding form has the following HTML code:

```
<form>
First Name: <input type="text" id="txt1"
  onkeyup="showHint(this.value)" />
</form>
<p>Suggestions: <span id="txtHint"></span></p>
```

It is just a simple HTML form with an input field called "txt1".

An event attribute for the input field defines a function to be triggered by the onkeyup event.

The paragraph below the form contains a span called "txtHint". The span is used as a placeholder for data retrieved from the Web server.

When a user inputs data, the function called "showHint()" is executed. The execution of the function is triggered by the "onkeyup" event. In other words, each time a user presses and then releases a key inside the input field, the function showHint is called.

The showHint() Function

The showHint() function is a very simple JavaScript function placed in the <head> section of the HTML page:

```
var xmlhttp;

function showHint(str)
{
if (str.length==0)
  {
  document.getElementById("txtHint").innerHTML="";
  return;
  }
xmlhttp=GetXmlHttpObject();
if (xmlhttp==null)
  {
  alert ("Your browser does not support XMLHTTP!");
  return;
  }
var url = "gethint.asp";
url = url + "?q =" +str;
url = url + "&sid=" +Math.random();
xmlhttp.onreadystatechange=stateChanged;
xmlhttp.open("GET",url,true);
xmlhttp.send(null);
}
```

The preceding function executes every time a character is entered in the input field.

If there is input in the input field (str.length > 0), the showHint() function executes the following:

▸▸ Defines the URL (*filename*) to send to the server

▸▸ Adds a parameter (*q*) to the URL with the content of the input field

▸▸ Adds a random number to prevent the server from using a cached file

▸▸ Creates an XMLHttp object and tells the object to execute a function called stateChanged when a change is triggered

▸▸ Opens the XMLHttp object with the given URL

▸▸ Sends an HTTP request to the server

If the input field is empty, the function simply clears the content of the txtHint placeholder.

The GetXmlHttpObject() Function

The showHint() function calls a function named GetXmlHttpObject().

The purpose of the GetXmlHttpObject() function is to solve the problem of creating different XMLHttp objects for different browsers:

```
function GetXmlHttpObject()
{
if (window.XMLHttpRequest)
  {
  // code for IE7+, Firefox, Chrome, Opera, Safari
  return new XMLHttpRequest();
  }
if (window.ActiveXObject)
  {
  // code for IE6, IE5
  return new ActiveXObject("Microsoft.XMLHTTP");
  }
return null;
}
```

The stateChanged() Function

The stateChanged() function contains the following code:

```
function stateChanged()
{
if (xmlhttp.readyState==4)
```

(continued)

(continued)

```
    {
    document.getElementById("txtHint").innerHTML=xmlhttp.re-
    sponseText;
    }
  }
```

The `stateChanged()` function executes every time the state of the XMLHttp object changes.

When the state changes to 4 ("complete"), the content of the `txtHint` placeholder is filled with the response text.

AJAX Suggest Source Code

The following source code belongs to the previous AJAX example.

You can copy and paste it, and try it yourself.

> **NOTE** Be sure to try it on a server with ASP or PHP enabled.

The AJAX HTML Page

This is the HTML page. It contains a simple HTML form and a link to a JavaScript.

```
<html>
<head>
<script src="clienthint.js"></script>
</head>
<body>

<form>
First Name: <input type="text" id="txt1"
  onkeyup="showHint(this.value)" />
</form>
<p>Suggestions: <span id="txtHint"></span></p>

</body>
</html>
```

The AJAX JavaScript

This is the JavaScript code, stored in the file clienthint.js:

```
var xmlhttp

function showHint(str)
{
if (str.length==0)
  {
  document.getElementById("txtHint").innerHTML="";
  return;
  }
xmlhttp=GetXmlHttpObject();
if (xmlhttp==null)
  {
  alert ("Your browser does not support XMLHTTP!");
  return;
  }
var url="gethint.asp";
url=url+"?q="+str;
url=url+"&sid="+Math.random();
xmlhttp.onreadystatechange=stateChanged;
xmlhttp.open("GET",url,true);
xmlhttp.send(null);
}

function stateChanged()
{
if (xmlhttp.readyState==4)
  {
  document.getElementById("txtHint").innerHTML=xmlhttp.re-
  sponseText;
  }
}

function GetXmlHttpObject()
{
if (window.XMLHttpRequest)
 {
  // code for IE7+, Firefox, Chrome, Opera, Safari
```

(continued)

(continued)

```
    return new XMLHttpRequest();
    }
  if (window.ActiveXObject)
    {
    // code for IE6, IE5
    return new ActiveXObject("Microsoft.XMLHTTP");
    }
  return null;
  }
```

The AJAX Server Page—ASP and PHP

There is no such thing as an AJAX server. AJAX pages can be served by any Internet server.

The server page called by the JavaScript in the previous example is a simple ASP file called gethint.asp.

Following are two examples of the server page code, one written in ASP and one in PHP.

AJAX ASP Example

The code in the gethint.asp page is written in VBScript for an Internet Information Server (IIS). It checks an array of names and returns the corresponding names to the client:

```
<%
response.expires=-1
dim a(30)
'Fill up array with names
a(1)="Anna"
a(2)="Brittany"
a(3)="Cinderella"
a(4)="Diana"
a(5)="Eva"
a(6)="Fiona"
a(7)="Gunda"
a(8)="Hege"
a(9)="Inga"
a(10)="Johanna"
a(11)="Kitty"
a(12)="Linda"
```

```
a(13)="Nina"
a(14)="Ophelia"
a(15)="Petunia"
a(16)="Amanda"
a(17)="Raquel"
a(18)="Cindy"
a(19)="Doris"
a(20)="Eve"
a(21)="Evita"
a(22)="Sunniva"
a(23)="Tove"
a(24)="Unni"
a(25)="Violet"
a(26)="Liza"
a(27)="Elizabeth"
a(28)="Ellen"
a(29)="Wenche"
a(30)="Vicky"

'get the q parameter from URL
q=ucase(request.querystring("q"))

'lookup all hints from array if length of q>0
if len(q)>0 then
  hint=""
  for i=1 to 30
    if q=ucase(mid(a(i),1,len(q))) then
      if hint="" then
        hint=a(i)
      else
        hint=hint & " , " & a(i)
      end if
    end if
  next
end if

'Output "no suggestion" if no hint were found
'or output the correct values
if hint="" then
  response.write("no suggestion")
else
```

(continued)

```
      response.write(hint)
    end if
    %>
```

AJAX PHP Example

The preceding code can be rewritten in PHP.

> **NOTE** To run the entire example in PHP, remember to change the value of the url variable in "clienthint.js" from "gethint.asp" to "gethint.php".

```php
<?php
// Fill up array with names
$a[]="Anna";
$a[]="Brittany";
$a[]="Cinderella";
$a[]="Diana";
$a[]="Eva";
$a[]="Fiona";
$a[]="Gunda";
$a[]="Hege";
$a[]="Inga";
$a[]="Johanna";
$a[]="Kitty";
$a[]="Linda";
$a[]="Nina";
$a[]="Ophelia";
$a[]="Petunia";
$a[]="Amanda";
$a[]="Raquel";
$a[]="Cindy";
$a[]="Doris";
$a[]="Eve";
$a[]="Evita";
$a[]="Sunniva";
$a[]="Tove";
$a[]="Unni";
$a[]="Violet";
$a[]="Liza";
$a[]="Elizabeth";
$a[]="Ellen";
```

```php
$a[]="Wenche";
$a[]="Vicky";

//get the q parameter from URL
$q=$_GET["q"];

//lookup all hints from array if length of q>0
if (strlen($q) > 0)
  {
  $hint="";
  for($i=0; $i<count($a); $i++)
    {
    if (strtolower($q)==strtolower(substr($a[$i],0,strlen(
  $q))))
      {
      if ($hint=="")
        {
        $hint=$a[$i];
        }
      else
        {
        $hint=$hint." , ".$a[$i];
        }
      }
    }
  }

// Set output to "no suggestion" if no hint were found
// or to the correct values
if ($hint == "")
  {
  $response="no suggestion";
  }
else
  {
  $response=$hint;
  }

//output the response
echo $response;
?>
```

CHAPTER 33

AJAX DATABASE EXAMPLE

In This Chapter

❑ The AJAX JavaScript

❑ The AJAX Server Page

AJAX can be used for interactive communication with a database.

The example shown in Figure 33.1 demonstrates how a Web page can fetch information from a database with AJAX technology.

Select a customer in the drop-down box below:

Select a Customer: Alfreds Futterkiste ▾

Customer info will be listed here.

Figure 33.1

The preceding example contains a simple HTML form and a link to a JavaScript:

```
<html>
<head>
<script type="text/javascript" src="selectcustomer.js"></
  script>
</head>

<body>

<form>
Select a Customer:
<select name="customers" onchange="showCustomer(this.
  value)">
```

```
<option value="ALFKI">Alfreds Futterkiste</option>
<option value="NORTS ">North/South</option>
<option value="WOLZA">Wolski Zajazd</option>
</select>
</form>

<div id="txtHint"><b>Customer info will be listed here.</
    b></div>

</body>
</html>
```

As you can see, it is just a simple HTML form with a drop-down box called customers.

The `<div>` below the form will be used as a placeholder for info retrieved from the Web server.

When the user selects data, a function called `showCustomer()` is executed. The execution of the function is triggered by the **"onchange"** event. In other words, each time the user changes the value in the drop-down box, the function `show-Customer()` is called.

The AJAX JavaScript

This is the JavaScript code stored in the file selectcustomer.js:

```
var xmlhttp

function showCustomer(str)
{
xmlhttp=GetXmlHttpObject();
if (xmlhttp==null)
  {
  alert ("Your browser does not support AJAX!");
  return;
  }
var url="getcustomer.asp";
url=url+"?q="+str;
url=url+"&sid="+Math.random();
xmlhttp.onreadystatechange=stateChanged;
xmlhttp.open("GET",url,true);
xmlhttp.send(null);
```

(continued)

(continued)

```
      }

      function stateChanged()
      {
      if (xmlhttp.readyState==4)
        {
        document.getElementById("txtHint").innerHTML=xmlhttp.
         responseText;
        }
      }

      function GetXmlHttpObject()
      {
      if (window.XMLHttpRequest)
        {
        // code for IE7+, Firefox, Chrome, Opera, Safari
        return new XMLHttpRequest();
        }
      if (window.ActiveXObject)
        {
        // code for IE6, IE5
        return new ActiveXObject("Microsoft.XMLHTTP");
        }
      return null;
      }
```

The AJAX Server Page

The server page called by the previous JavaScript script is an ASP file called getcustomer.asp.

The ASP page is written in VBScript for an Internet Information Server (IIS). It could easily be rewritten in PHP or some other server language.

The code runs a query against a database and returns the result in an HTML table:

```
<%
response.expires=-1
sql="SELECT * FROM CUSTOMERS WHERE CUSTOMERID="
sql=sql & "'" & request.querystring("q") & "'"
```

```
set conn=Server.CreateObject("ADODB.Connection")
conn.Provider="Microsoft.Jet.OLEDB.4.0"
conn.Open(Server.Mappath("/db/northwind.mdb"))
set rs=Server.CreateObject("ADODB.recordset")
rs.Open sql,conn

response.write("<table>")
do until rs.EOF
  for each x in rs.Fields
    response.write("<tr><td><b>" & x.name & "</b></td>")
    response.write("<td>" & x.value & "</td></tr>")
  next
  rs.MoveNext
loop

response.write("</table>")
%>
```

CHAPTER 34

AJAX XML EXAMPLE

In This Chapter

❑ The AJAX JavaScript

❑ The AJAX Server Page

❑ The XML File

AJAX can be used for interactive communication with an XML file.

The example in Figure 34.1 demonstrates how a Web page can fetch information from an XML file with AJAX technology.

Select a cd in the drop-down box below:

Select a CD: Bob Dylan ▾

CD info will be listed here...

Figure 34.1

The preceding example contains a simple HTML form and a link to a JavaScript:

```
<html>
<head>
<script src="selectcd.js"></script>
</head>

<body>

<form>
Select a CD:
<select name="cds" onchange="showCD(this.value)">
<option value="Bob Dylan">Bob Dylan</option>
<option value="Bonnie Tyler">Bonnie Tyler</option>
<option value="Dolly Parton">Dolly Parton</option>
```

```
</select>
</form>

<div id="txtHint"><b>CD info will be listed here.</b></div>

</body>
</html>
```

As you can see, it is just a simple HTML form with a simple drop-down box called cds.

The <div> below the form will be used as a placeholder for info retrieved from the Web server.

When the user selects data, a function called showCD is executed. The execution of the function is triggered by the onchange event. In other words each time the user changes the value in the drop-down box, the function showCD is called.

The AJAX JavaScript

This is the JavaScript code stored in the file selectcd.js:

```
var xmlhttp

function showCD(str)
{
xmlhttp=GetXmlHttpObject();
if (xmlhttp==null)
  {
  alert ("Your browser does not support AJAX!");
  return;
  }
var url="getcd.asp";
url=url+"?q="+str;
url=url+"&sid="+Math.random();
xmlhttp.onreadystatechange=stateChanged;
xmlhttp.open("GET",url,true);
xmlhttp.send(null);
}

function stateChanged()
{
```

(continued)

(continued)

```
    if (xmlhttp.readyState==4)
    {
    document.getElementById("txtHint").innerHTML=xmlhttp.
      responseText;
    }
    }

    function GetXmlHttpObject()
    {
    if (window.XMLHttpRequest)
      {
      // code for IE7+, Firefox, Chrome, Opera, Safari
      return new XMLHttpRequest();
      }
    if (window.ActiveXObject)
      {
      // code for IE6, IE5
      return new ActiveXObject("Microsoft.XMLHTTP");
      }
    return null;
    }
```

The AJAX Server Page

The server page called by the preceding JavaScript is an ASP file called getcd.asp.

The page is written in VBScript for an Internet Information Server (IIS). It could easily be rewritten in PHP or some other server language.

The code runs a query against an XML file and returns the result as HTML:

```
<%
response.expires=-1
q=request.querystring("q")

set xmlDoc=Server.CreateObject("Microsoft.XMLDOM")
xmlDoc.async="false"
xmlDoc.load(Server.MapPath("cd_catalog.xml"))

set nodes=xmlDoc.selectNodes("CATALOG/CD[ARTIST='" & q &
  "']")
```

```
for each x in nodes
  for each y in x.childnodes
    response.write("<b>" & y.nodename & ":</b> ")
    response.write(y.text)
    response.write("<br />")
  next
next
%>
```

The XML File

The XML file used in the example is cd_catalog.xml. This document contains a CD collection and appears as follows:

```
<!-- Edited by XMLSpy® -->
-
<CATALOG>
-
<CD>
<TITLE>Empire Burlesque</TITLE>
<ARTIST>Bob Dylan</ARTIST>
<COUNTRY>USA</COUNTRY>
<COMPANY>Columbia</COMPANY>
<PRICE>10.90</PRICE>
<YEAR>1985</YEAR>
</CD>
-
<CD>
<TITLE>Hide your heart</TITLE>
<ARTIST>Bonnie Tyler</ARTIST>
<COUNTRY>UK</COUNTRY>
<COMPANY>CBS Records</COMPANY>
<PRICE>9.90</PRICE>
<YEAR>1988</YEAR>
</CD>
-
<CD>
<TITLE>Greatest Hits</TITLE>
<ARTIST>Dolly Parton</ARTIST>
<COUNTRY>USA</COUNTRY>
```

(continued)

191

(continued)

```
        <COMPANY>RCA</COMPANY>
        <PRICE>9.90</PRICE>
        <YEAR>1982</YEAR>
        </CD>
        -
        <CD>
        <TITLE>Still got the blues</TITLE>
        <ARTIST>Gary Moore</ARTIST>
        <COUNTRY>UK</COUNTRY>
        <COMPANY>Virgin records</COMPANY>
        <PRICE>10.20</PRICE>
        <YEAR>1990</YEAR>
        </CD>
        -
        <CD>
        <TITLE>Eros</TITLE>
        <ARTIST>Eros Ramazzotti</ARTIST>
        <COUNTRY>EU</COUNTRY>
        <COMPANY>BMG</COMPANY>
        <PRICE>9.90</PRICE>
        <YEAR>1997</YEAR>
        </CD>
        -
        <CD>
        <TITLE>One night only</TITLE>
        <ARTIST>Bee Gees</ARTIST>
        <COUNTRY>UK</COUNTRY>
        <COMPANY>Polydor</COMPANY>
        <PRICE>10.90</PRICE>
        <YEAR>1998</YEAR>
        </CD>
        -
        <CD>
        <TITLE>Sylvias Mother</TITLE>
        <ARTIST>Dr.Hook</ARTIST>
        <COUNTRY>UK</COUNTRY>
        <COMPANY>CBS</COMPANY>
        <PRICE>8.10</PRICE>
        <YEAR>1973</YEAR>
        </CD>
```

```
–
<CD>
<TITLE>Maggie May</TITLE>
<ARTIST>Rod Stewart</ARTIST>
<COUNTRY>UK</COUNTRY>
<COMPANY>Pickwick</COMPANY>
<PRICE>8.50</PRICE>
<YEAR>1990</YEAR>
</CD>
–
<CD>
<TITLE>Romanza</TITLE>
<ARTIST>Andrea Bocelli</ARTIST>
<COUNTRY>EU</COUNTRY>
<COMPANY>Polydor</COMPANY>
<PRICE>10.80</PRICE>
<YEAR>1996</YEAR>
</CD>
–
<CD>
<TITLE>When a man loves a woman</TITLE>
<ARTIST>Percy Sledge</ARTIST>
<COUNTRY>USA</COUNTRY>
<COMPANY>Atlantic</COMPANY>
<PRICE>8.70</PRICE>
<YEAR>1987</YEAR>
</CD>
–
<CD>
<TITLE>Black angel</TITLE>
<ARTIST>Savage Rose</ARTIST>
<COUNTRY>EU</COUNTRY>
<COMPANY>Mega</COMPANY>
<PRICE>10.90</PRICE>
<YEAR>1995</YEAR>
</CD>
–
<CD>
<TITLE>1999 Grammy Nominees</TITLE>
<ARTIST>Many</ARTIST>
```

(continued)

(continued)

```
        <COUNTRY>USA</COUNTRY>
        <COMPANY>Grammy</COMPANY>
        <PRICE>10.20</PRICE>
        <YEAR>1999</YEAR>
        </CD>
        –
        <CD>
        <TITLE>For the good times</TITLE>
        <ARTIST>Kenny Rogers</ARTIST>
        <COUNTRY>UK</COUNTRY>
        <COMPANY>Mucik Master</COMPANY>
        <PRICE>8.70</PRICE>
        <YEAR>1995</YEAR>
        </CD>
        –
        <CD>
        <TITLE>Big Willie style</TITLE>
        <ARTIST>Will Smith</ARTIST>
        <COUNTRY>USA</COUNTRY>
        <COMPANY>Columbia</COMPANY>
        <PRICE>9.90</PRICE>
        <YEAR>1997</YEAR>
        </CD>
        –
        <CD>
        <TITLE>Tupelo Honey</TITLE>
        <ARTIST>Van Morrison</ARTIST>
        <COUNTRY>UK</COUNTRY>
        <COMPANY>Polydor</COMPANY>
        <PRICE>8.20</PRICE>
        <YEAR>1971</YEAR>
        </CD>
        –
        <CD>
        <TITLE>Soulsville</TITLE>
        <ARTIST>Jorn Hoel</ARTIST>
        <COUNTRY>Norway</COUNTRY>
        <COMPANY>WEA</COMPANY>
        <PRICE>7.90</PRICE>
        <YEAR>1996</YEAR>
```

```
</CD>
-
<CD>
<TITLE>The very best of</TITLE>
<ARTIST>Cat Stevens</ARTIST>
<COUNTRY>UK</COUNTRY>
<COMPANY>Island</COMPANY>
<PRICE>8.90</PRICE>
<YEAR>1990</YEAR>
</CD>
-
<CD>
<TITLE>Stop</TITLE>
<ARTIST>Sam Brown</ARTIST>
<COUNTRY>UK</COUNTRY>
<COMPANY>A and M</COMPANY>
<PRICE>8.90</PRICE>
<YEAR>1988</YEAR>
</CD>
-
<CD>
<TITLE>Bridge of Spies</TITLE>
<ARTIST>T'Pau</ARTIST>
<COUNTRY>UK</COUNTRY>
<COMPANY>Siren</COMPANY>
<PRICE>7.90</PRICE>
<YEAR>1987</YEAR>
</CD>
-
<CD>
<TITLE>Private Dancer</TITLE>
<ARTIST>Tina Turner</ARTIST>
<COUNTRY>UK</COUNTRY>
<COMPANY>Capitol</COMPANY>
<PRICE>8.90</PRICE>
<YEAR>1983</YEAR>
</CD>
-
<CD>
<TITLE>Midt om natten</TITLE>
```

(continued)

195

(continued)

```
        <ARTIST>Kim Larsen</ARTIST>
        <COUNTRY>EU</COUNTRY>
        <COMPANY>Medley</COMPANY>
        <PRICE>7.80</PRICE>
        <YEAR>1983</YEAR>
        </CD>
        −
        <CD>
        <TITLE>Pavarotti Gala Concert</TITLE>
        <ARTIST>Luciano Pavarotti</ARTIST>
        <COUNTRY>UK</COUNTRY>
        <COMPANY>DECCA</COMPANY>
        <PRICE>9.90</PRICE>
        <YEAR>1991</YEAR>
        </CD>
        −
        <CD>
        <TITLE>The dock of the bay</TITLE>
        <ARTIST>Otis Redding</ARTIST>
        <COUNTRY>USA</COUNTRY>
        <COMPANY>Atlantic</COMPANY>
        <PRICE>7.90</PRICE>
        <YEAR>1987</YEAR>
        </CD>
        −
        <CD>
        <TITLE>Picture book</TITLE>
        <ARTIST>Simply Red</ARTIST>
        <COUNTRY>EU</COUNTRY>
        <COMPANY>Elektra</COMPANY>
        <PRICE>7.20</PRICE>
        <YEAR>1985</YEAR>
        </CD>
        −
        <CD>
        <TITLE>Red</TITLE>
        <ARTIST>The Communards</ARTIST>
        <COUNTRY>UK</COUNTRY>
        <COMPANY>London</COMPANY>
        <PRICE>7.80</PRICE>
```

```
<YEAR>1987</YEAR>
</CD>
-
<CD>
<TITLE>Unchain my heart</TITLE>
<ARTIST>Joe Cocker</ARTIST>
<COUNTRY>USA</COUNTRY>
<COMPANY>EMI</COMPANY>
<PRICE>8.20</PRICE>
<YEAR>1987</YEAR>
</CD>
</CATALOG>
```

CHAPTER 35

AJAX RESPONSEXML EXAMPLE

In This Chapter

❏ The AJAX JavaScript

❏ The AJAX Server Page

responseText returns the HTTP response as a string.

responseXML returns the response as XML.

The responseXML property returns an XML document object, which can be examined and parsed using the DOM (Document Object Model).

 See Appendix B for a complete listing of the HTML DOM Objects.

The example in Figure 35.1 demonstrates how a Web page can fetch information from a database with AJAX technology. The selected data from the database will this time be converted to an XML document, and then we will use the DOM to extract the values to be displayed.

Select a customer: Alfreds Futterkiste ▾

Figure 35.1

The preceding example contains an HTML form, several `<span>` elements to hold the returned data, and a link to a JavaScript:

```
<html>
<head>
<script src="selectcustomer_xml.js"></script>
</head>
<body>

<form action="">
Select a Customer:
```

198

```
<select name="customers" onchange="showCustomer(this.
  value)">
<option value="ALFKI">Alfreds Futterkiste</option>
<option value="NORTS ">North/South</option>
<option value="WOLZA">Wolski Zajazd</option>
</select>
</form>

<b><span id="companyname"></span></b><br />
<span id="contactname"></span><br />
<span id="address"></span>
<span id="city"></span><br/>
<span id="country"></span>


</body>
</html>
```

The preceding example contains an HTML form with a drop-down box called customers.

When the user selects a customer in the drop-down box, a function called showCustomer() is executed. The execution of the function is triggered by the onchange event. In other words. each time the user changes the value in the drop-down box, the function showCustomer() is called.

The AJAX JavaScript

This is the JavaScript code stored in the file selectcustomer_xml.js:

```
var xmlhttp

function showCustomer(str)
{
xmlhttp=GetXmlHttpObject();
if (xmlhttp==null)
  {
  alert ("Your browser does not support AJAX!");
  return;
  }
var url="getcustomer_xml.asp";
url=url+"?q="+str;
url=url+"&sid="+Math.random();
```

(continued)

(continued)

```
    xmlhttp.onreadystatechange=stateChanged;
    xmlhttp.open("GET",url,true);
    xmlhttp.send(null);
    }

    function stateChanged()
    {
    if (xmlhttp.readyState==4)
      {
      var xmlDoc=xmlhttp.responseXML.documentElement;
      document.getElementById("companyname").innerHTML=
      xmlDoc.getElementsByTagName("compname")[0].childNodes[0].
      nodeValue;
      document.getElementById("contactname").innerHTML=
      xmlDoc.getElementsByTagName("contname")[0].childNodes[0].
      nodeValue;
      document.getElementById("address").innerHTML=
      xmlDoc.getElementsByTagName("address")[0].childNodes[0].
      nodeValue;
      document.getElementById("city").innerHTML=
      xmlDoc.getElementsByTagName("city")[0].childNodes[0].node-
      Value;
      document.getElementById("country").innerHTML=
      xmlDoc.getElementsByTagName("country")[0].childNodes[0].
      nodeValue;
      }
    }

    function GetXmlHttpObject()
    {
    if (window.XMLHttpRequest)
      {
      // code for IE7+, Firefox, Chrome, Opera, Safari
      return new XMLHttpRequest();
      }
    if (window.ActiveXObject)
      {
      // code for IE6, IE5
      return new ActiveXObject("Microsoft.XMLHTTP");
      }
    return null;
    }
```

The `showCustomer()` and `GetXmlHttpObject()` functions are the same as in previous chapters. The `stateChanged()` function also is used earlier in this tutorial; however, this time we return the result as an XML document (with **response XML**) and use the DOM to extract the values we want to be displayed.

The AJAX Server Page

The server page called by the JavaScript is an ASP file called getcustomer_xml.asp.

The page is written in VBScript for an Internet Information Server (IIS). It could easily be rewritten in PHP or some other server language.

The code runs a query against a database and returns the result as an XML document:

```
<%
response.expires=-1
response.contenttype="text/xml"

sql="SELECT * FROM CUSTOMERS "
sql=sql & " WHERE CUSTOMERID='" & request.querystring("q") &
"'"

on error resume next
set conn=Server.CreateObject("ADODB.Connection")
conn.Provider="Microsoft.Jet.OLEDB.4.0"
conn.Open(Server.Mappath("/db/northwind.mdb"))
set rs=Server.CreateObject("ADODB.recordset")
rs.Open sql, conn

if err <> 0 then
  response.write(err.description)
  set rs=nothing
  set conn=nothing
else
  response.write("<?xml version='1.0'
  encoding='ISO-8859-1'?>")
  response.write("<company>")
  response.write("<compname>" &rs.fields("companyname")& "</
  compname>")
  response.write("<contname>" &rs.fields("contactname")& "</
  contname>")
  response.write("<address>" &rs.fields("address")& "
  </address>")
```

(continued)

(continued)

```
        response.write("<city>" &rs.fields("city")& "</city>")
        response.write("<country>" &rs.fields("country")& "
        </country>")
        response.write("</company>")
    end if
    on error goto 0
    %>
```

Notice the second line in the ASP code: `response.contenttype="text/xml"`. The `ContentType` property sets the HTTP content type for the response object. The default value for this property is "`text/html`". This time we want the content type to be XML.

Then we select data from the database and build an XML document with the data.

JAVASCRIPT OBJECTS

In This Appendix

- ❏ Array Object
- ❏ Boolean Object
- ❏ Date Object
- ❏ Math Object
- ❏ Number Object
- ❏ String Object
- ❏ RegExp Object
- ❏ Global Properties and Functions

Array Object

The Array object is used to store multiple values in a single variable.

 For a tutorial about arrays, see Chapter 17, "JavaScript Array Object."

Array Object Properties

Property	Description
constructor	Returns the function that created the Array object's prototype
length	Sets or returns the number of elements in an array
prototype	Allows you to add properties and methods to an object

Array Object Methods

Method	Description
concat()	Joins two or more arrays, and returns a copy of the joined arrays
join()	Joins all elements of an array into a string
pop()	Removes the last element of an array, and returns that element
push()	Adds new elements to the end of an array, and returns the new length
reverse()	Reverses the order of the elements in an array
shift()	Removes the first element of an array, and returns that element
slice()	Selects a part of an array, and returns the new array
sort()	Sorts the elements of an array
splice()	Adds/Removes elements from an array
toString()	Converts an array to a string, and returns the result
unshift()	Adds new elements to the beginning of an array, and returns the new length
valueOf()	Returns the primitive value of an array as values separated by commas

Boolean Object

The Boolean object is used to convert a non-Boolean value to a Boolean value (true or false).

For a tutorial about the Boolean object, see Chapter 18, "JavaScript Boolean Object."

Boolean Object Properties

Property	Description
constructor	Returns the function that created the Boolean object's prototype
prototype	Allows you to add properties and methods to an object

Boolean Object Methods

Method	Description
toString()	Converts a Boolean value to a string, and returns the result
valueOf()	Returns the primitive value of a Boolean object

Date Object

The Date object is used to work with dates and times.

Date objects are created with new `Date()`.

There are four ways of instantiating a date:

```
var d = new Date();
```

```
var d = new Date(milliseconds);
var d = new Date(dateString);
var d = new Date(year, month, day, hours, minutes, seconds,
    milliseconds);
```

For a tutorial about date and times, see Chapter 16, "JavaScript Date Object."

Date Object Properties

Property	Description
constructor	Returns the function that created the Date object's prototype
prototype	Allows you to add properties and methods to an object

Date Object Methods

Method	Description
getDate()	Returns the day of the month (from 1–31)
getDay()	Returns the day of the week (from 0–6)
getFullYear()	Returns the year (four digits)
getHours()	Returns the hour (from 0–23)
getMilliseconds()	Returns the milliseconds (from 0–999)
getMinutes()	Returns the minutes (from 0–59)
getMonth()	Returns the month (from 0–11)
getSeconds()	Returns the seconds (from 0–59)
getTime()	Returns the number of milliseconds since midnight January 1, 1970
getTimezoneOffset()	Returns the time difference between GMT and local time in minutes
getUTCDate()	Returns the day of the month, according to universal time (from 1–31)
getUTCDay()	Returns the day of the week, according to universal time (from 0–6)
getUTCFullYear()	Returns the year, according to universal time (four digits)
getUTCHours()	Returns the hour, according to universal time (from 0–23)
getUTCMilliseconds()	Returns the milliseconds, according to universal time (from 0–999)
getUTCMinutes()	Returns the minutes, according to universal time (from 0–59)
getUTCMonth()	Returns the month, according to universal time (from 0–11)
getUTCSeconds()	Returns the seconds, according to universal time (from 0–59)
getYear()	Deprecated. Use the getFullYear() method instead
parse()	Parses a date string and returns the number of milliseconds since midnight of January 1, 1970
setDate()	Sets the day of the month (from 1–31)

(continued)

205

(continued)

Method	Description
setFullYear()	Sets the year (four digits)
setHours()	Sets the hour (from 0–23)
setMilliseconds()	Sets the milliseconds (from 0–999)
setMinutes()	Set the minutes (from 0–59)
setMonth()	Sets the month (from 0–11)
setSeconds()	Sets the seconds (from 0–59)
setTime()	Sets a date and time by adding or subtracting a specified number of milliseconds to/from midnight January 1, 1970
setUTCDate()	Sets the day of the month, according to universal time (from 1–31)
setUTCFullYear()	Sets the year, according to universal time (four digits)
setUTCHours()	Sets the hour, according to universal time (from 0–23)
setUTCMilliseconds()	Sets the milliseconds, according to universal time (from 0–999)
setUTCMinutes()	Set the minutes, according to universal time (from 0–59)
setUTCMonth()	Sets the month, according to universal time (from 0–11)
setUTCSeconds()	Set the seconds, according to universal time (from 0–59)
setYear()	Deprecated. Use the setFullYear() method instead
toDateString()	Converts the date portion of a Date object into a readable string
toGMTString()	Deprecated. Use the toUTCString() method instead
toLocaleDateString()	Returns the date portion of a Date object as a string, using locale conventions
toLocaleTimeString()	Returns the time portion of a Date object as a string, using locale conventions
toLocaleString()	Converts a Date object to a string, using locale conventions
toString()	Converts a Date object to a string
toTimeString()	Converts the time portion of a Date object to a string
toUTCString()	Converts a Date object to a string, according to universal time
UTC()	Returns the number of milliseconds in a date string since midnight of January 1, 1970, according to universal time
valueOf()	Converts a Date to milliseconds. Same as `getTime()`.

Math Object

The Math object allows you to perform mathematical tasks.

Math is not a constructor. All properties/methods of Math can be called by using Math as an object, without creating it.

The syntax is as follows:

```
var x = Math.PI; // Returns PI
var y = Math.sqrt(16); // Returns the square root of 16
```

For a tutorial about the Math object, see Chapter 19, "JavaScript Math Object."

Math Object Properties

Property	Description
E	Returns Euler's number, the base of the natural logarithm (approx. 2.718)
LN2	Returns the natural logarithm of 2 (approx. 0.693)
LN10	Returns the natural logarithm of 10 (approx. 2.302)
LOG2E	Returns the base-2 logarithm of E (approx. 1.442)
LOG10E	Returns the base-10 logarithm of E (approx. 0.434)
PI	Returns PI (approx. 3.14159)
SQRT1_2	Returns the square root of 1/2 (approx. 0.707)
SQRT2	Returns the square root of 2 (approx. 1.414)

Math Object Methods

Method	Description
abs(x)	Returns the absolute value of x
acos(x)	Returns the arccosine of x, in radians
asin(x)	Returns the arcsine of x, in radians
atan(x)	Returns the arctangent of x as a numeric value between $-PI/2$ and $PI/2$ radians
atan2(y,x)	Returns the arctangent of the quotient of its arguments
ceil(x)	Returns x, rounded upward to the nearest integer
cos(x)	Returns the cosine of x (x is in radians)
exp(x)	Returns the value of E to the power of x
floor(x)	Returns x, rounded downward to the nearest integer
log(x)	Returns the natural logarithm (base E) of x
max(x,y,z,...,n)	Returns the number with the highest value
min(x,y,z,...,n)	Returns the number with the lowest value
pow(x,y)	Returns the value of x to the power of y
random()	Returns a random number between 0 and 1
round(x)	Rounds x to the nearest integer
sin(x)	Returns the sine of x (x is in radians)
sqrt(x)	Returns the square root of x
tan(x)	Returns the tangent of x (x is in radians)

Number Object

The Number object is an object wrapper for primitive numeric values.

Number objects are created with new `Number()`.

The syntax is as follows:

```
var num = new Number(value);
```

> **NOTE** If the value parameter cannot be converted into a number, it returns NaN (Not-a-Number).

Number Object Properties

Property	Description
constructor	Returns the function that created the Number object's prototype
MAX_VALUE	Returns the largest number possible in JavaScript
MIN_VALUE	Returns the smallest number possible in JavaScript
NEGATIVE _INFINITY	Represents negative infinity (returned on overflow)
POSITIVE_INFINITY	Represents infinity (returned on overflow)
prototype	Allows you to add properties and methods to an object

Number Object Methods

Method	Description
toExponential(x)	Converts a number to exponential notation
toFixed(x)	Formats a number with x number of digits after the decimal point
toPrecision(x)	Formats a number to x significant digits
toString()	Converts a Number object to a string
valueOf()	Returns the primitive value of a Number object

String Object

The String object is used to manipulate a stored piece of text.

String objects are created with new String().

The syntax is as follows:

```
var txt = new String(string);
```
or more simply:

```
var txt = string;
```

For a tutorial about the String object, see Chapter 15, "JavaScript String Object."

String Object Properties

Property	Description
constructor	Returns the function that created the String object's prototype
length	Returns the length of a string
prototype	Allows you to add properties and methods to an object

String Object Methods

Method	Description
charAt()	Returns the character at the specified index
charCodeAt()	Returns the Unicode of the character at the specified index
concat()	Joins two or more strings, and returns a copy of the joined strings
fromCharCode()	Converts Unicode values to characters
indexOf()	Returns the position of the first found occurrence of a specified value in a string
lastIndexOf()	Returns the position of the last found occurrence of a specified value in a string
match()	Searches for a match within the string using a regular expression. Returns an array or null if no matches found.
replace()	Searches for a match between a substring (or regular expression) and a string, and replaces the matched substring with a new substring
search()	Searches for a match between a regular expression and a string, and returns the position of the match or −1 if not found
slice()	Extracts a part of a string and returns a new string
split()	Splits a string into an array of substrings
substr()	Extracts the characters from a string, beginning at a specified start position through the specified number of characters
substring()	Extracts the characters from a string, between two specified indices
toLowerCase()	Converts a string to lowercase letters
toUpperCase()	Converts a string to uppercase letters
valueOf()	Returns the primitive value of a String object

String HTML Wrapper Methods

The HTML wrapper methods return the string wrapped inside the appropriate HTML tag.

Method	Description
anchor()	Creates an anchor
big()	Displays a string using a big font
blink()	Displays a blinking string
bold()	Displays a string in bold
fixed()	Displays a string using a fixed-pitch font
fontcolor()	Displays a string using a specified color
fontsize()	Displays a string using a specified size
italics()	Displays a string in italic
link()	Displays a string as a hyperlink
small()	Displays a string using a small font
strike()	Displays a string with a strikethrough
sub()	Displays a string as subscript text
sup()	Displays a string as superscript text

RegExp Object

A regular expression is an object that describes a pattern of characters.

Regular expressions are used to perform pattern-matching and search-and-replace functions on text.

The syntax is as follows:

```
var txt=new RegExp(pattern,modifiers);
```

or more simply:

```
var txt=/pattern/modifiers;
```

▶▶ Pattern specifies the pattern of an expression.

▶▶ Modifiers specify whether a search should be global, case-sensitive, and so on.

For a tutorial about the RegExp object, see Chapter 20, "JavaScript RegExp Object."

Modifiers

Modifiers are used to perform case-insensitive and global searches:

Modifier	Description
i	Perform case-insensitive matching
g	Perform a global match (find all matches rather than stopping after the first match)
m	Perform multiline matching

Brackets

Brackets are used to find a range of characters:

Expression	Description
[abc]	Match any character between the brackets
[^abc]	Match any character not between the brackets
[0-9]	Match any digit from 0 to 9
[a-z]	Match any character from lowercase a to lowercase z
[A-Z]	Match any character from uppercase A to uppercase Z
[a-Z]	Match any character from lowercase a to uppercase Z
[adgk]	Match any character in the given set
[^adgk]	Match any character outside the given set
[red|blue|green]	Match any of the alternatives specified

Metacharacters

Metacharacters are characters with a special meaning:

Metacharacter	Description
.	Find a single character, except newline or line terminator
\w	Match any alphanumeric character, including the underscore
\W	Match any nonalphanumeric character
\d	Find a digit
\D	Find a nondigit character
\s	Find a single whitespace character
\S	Find a single nonwhitespace character
\b	Match at the beginning/end of a word
\B	Match not at the beginning/end of a word
\0	Find a NUL character
\n	Find a new line
\f	Find a form feed
\r	Find a carriage return
\t	Find a tab
\v	Find a vertical tab
\xxx	Find the character specified by an octal number xxx
\xdd	Find the character specified by a hexadecimal number dd
\uxxxx	Find the Unicode character specified by a hexadecimal number *xxxx*

Quantifiers

Quantifier	Description
+	Match the preceding character 1 or more times
*	Match the preceding character 0 or more times
?	Match the preceding character 0 or 1 time
{x}	Where x is a positive integer, matches exactly n occurrences of the preceding character
{x,y}	Where x and y are positive integers, matches at least x and no more than y occurrences of the preceding character
{x,}	Where x is a positive integer, matches at least n occurrences of the preceding character
n$	Matches any string with *n* at the end of it
^n	Matches any string with *n* at the beginning of it
n(?=m)	Matches n only if followed by *m*
n(?|m)	Matches n only if not followed by *m*

RegExp Object Properties

Property	Description
global	Specifies if the "g" modifier is set
ignoreCase	Specifies if the "i" modifier is set
lastIndex	The index at which to start the next match
multiline	Specifies if the "m" modifier is set
source	The text of the RegExp pattern

RegExp Object Methods

Method	Description
compile()	Compiles a regular expression
exec()	Tests for a match in a string. Returns a result array
test()	Tests for a match in a string. Returns true or false

JavaScript Global Properties and Functions

The JavaScript global properties and functions can be used with all the built-in JavaScript objects.

JavaScript Global Properties

Property	Description
Infinity	A numeric value that represents positive/negative infinity
NaN	"Not-a-Number" value
undefined	Indicates that a variable has not been assigned a value

JavaScript Global Functions

Function	Description
decodeURI()	Decodes a URI
decodeURIComponent()	Decodes a URI component
encodeURI()	Encodes a URI
encodeURIComponent()	Encodes a URI component
escape()	Encodes a string
eval()	Evaluates a string and executes it as if it were a JavaScript expression
isFinite()	Determines whether a value is a finite number
isNaN()	Determines whether a value is an illegal number
Number()	Converts an object's value to a number

Function	Description
parseFloat()	Parses a string and returns a floating point number
parseInt()	Parses a string and returns an integer
String()	Converts an object's value to a string
unescape()	Decodes an encoded string

HTML DOM OBJECTS

In This Appendix

- ❑ Document Object
- ❑ Event Object
- ❑ Element Object
- ❑ Anchor Object
- ❑ Area Object
- ❑ Base Object
- ❑ Body Object
- ❑ Button Object (Push Button)
- ❑ Form Object
- ❑ Frame/IFrame Object
- ❑ Frameset Object
- ❑ Image Object
- ❑ Button Object
- ❑ Checkbox Object
- ❑ FileUpload Object
- ❑ Hidden Object
- ❑ Password Object
- ❑ Radio Object
- ❑ Reset Object
- ❑ Submit Object
- ❑ Text Object

❑ Link Object

❑ Meta Object

❑ Object Object

❑ Option Object

❑ Select Object

❑ Style Object

❑ Table Object

❑ TableCell Object

❑ TableRow Object

❑ Textarea Object

The World Wide Web Consortium (W3C) is an international community that develops **standards** to ensure the long-term growth of the Web. The W3C DOM page is located at http://www.w3.org/DOM/.

Document Object

Each HTML document loaded into a browser window becomes a Document object.

The Document object provides access to all HTML elements in a page, from within a script.

> TIP   The Document object is also part of the Window object and can be accessed through the `window.document` property.

Document Object Collections

W3C: W3C Standard

Collection	Description	W3C
anchors[]	Returns an array of all the anchors in the document	Yes
forms[]	Returns an array of all the forms in the document	Yes
images[]	Returns an array of all the images in the document	Yes
links[]	Returns an array of all the links in the document	Yes

Document Object Properties

Property	Description	W3C
cookie	Returns all name/value pairs of cookies in the document	Yes
documentMode	Returns the mode used by the browser to render the document	No
domain	Returns the domain name of the server that loaded the document	Yes
lastModified	Returns the date and time the document was last modified	No
readyState	Returns the (loading) status of the document	No
referrer	Returns the URL of the document that loaded the current document	Yes
title	Sets or returns the title of the document	Yes
URL	Returns the full URL of the document	Yes

Document Object Methods

Method	Description	W3C
close()	Closes the output stream previously opened with document.open()	Yes
getElementById()	Accesses the first element with the specified id	Yes
getElementsByName()	Accesses all elements with a specified name	Yes
getElementsByTagName()	Accesses all elements with a specified tagname	Yes
open()	Opens an output stream to collect the output from document.write() or document.writeln()	Yes
write()	Writes HTML expressions or JavaScript code to a document	Yes
writeln()	Same as write(), but adds a newline character after each statement	Yes

Event Object

The Event object gives you information about an event that has occurred.

The Event object represents the state of an event, such as the element in which the event occurred, the state of the keyboard keys, the location of the mouse, and the state of the mouse buttons.

Events are normally used in combination with functions, and the function will not be executed before the event occurs!

Event Handlers

New to HTML 4.0 was the ability to let HTML events trigger actions in the browser, like starting a JavaScript when a user clicks on an HTML element. Following is a list of the attributes that can be inserted into HTML tags to define event actions.

IE: Internet Explorer; F: Firefox; O: Opera; W3C: W3C Standard.

Attribute	The event occurs when...	IE	F	O	W3C
onblur	An element loses focus	3	1	9	Yes
onchange	The content of a field changes	3	1	9	Yes
onclick	Mouse clicks an object	3	1	9	Yes
ondblclick	Mouse double-clicks an object	4	1	9	Yes
onerror	An error occurs when loading a document or an image	4	1	9	Yes
onfocus	An element gets focus	3	1	9	Yes
onkeydown	A keyboard key is pressed	3	1	No	Yes
onkeypress	A keyboard key is pressed or held down	3	1	9	Yes
onkeyup	A keyboard key is released	3	1	9	Yes
onload	A page or an image is finished loading	3	1	9	Yes
onmousedown	A mouse button is pressed	4	1	9	Yes
onmousemove	The mouse is moved	3	1	9	Yes
onmouseout	The mouse is moved off an element	4	1	9	Yes
onmouseover	The mouse is moved over an element	3	1	9	Yes
onmouseup	A mouse button is released	4	1	9	Yes
onresize	A window or frame is resized	4	1	9	Yes
onselect	Text is selected	3	1	9	Yes
onunload	The user exits the page	3	1	9	Yes

Mouse / Keyboard Attributes

Property	Description	IE	F	O	W3C
altKey	Returns whether the Alt key was pressed when an event was triggered	6	1	9	Yes
button	Returns which mouse button was clicked when an event was triggered	6	1	9	Yes
clientX	Returns the horizontal coordinate of the mouse pointer when an event was triggered	6	1	9	Yes
clientY	Returns the vertical coordinate of the mouse pointer when an event was triggered	6	1	9	Yes
ctrlKey	Returns whether the Ctrl key was pressed when an event was triggered	6	1	9	Yes
metaKey	Returns whether the meta key was pressed when an event was triggered	6	1	9	Yes
relatedTarget	Returns the element related to the element that triggered the event	No	1	9	Yes
screenX	Returns the horizontal coordinate of the mouse pointer when an event was triggered	6	1	9	Yes
screenY	Returns the vertical coordinate of the mouse pointer when an event was triggered	6	1	9	Yes
shiftKey	Returns whether the Shift key was pressed when an event was triggered	6	1	9	Yes

Other Event Attributes

Property	Description	IE	F	O	W3C
bubbles	Returns a Boolean value that indicates whether an event is a bubbling event	No	1	9	Yes
cancelable	Returns a Boolean value that indicates whether an event can have its default action prevented	No	1	9	Yes
currentTarget	Returns the element whose event listeners triggered the event	No	1	9	Yes
eventPhase	Returns which phase of the event flow is currently being evaluated				Yes
target	Returns the element that triggered the event	No	1	9	Yes
timeStamp	Returns the time stamp, in milliseconds, from the epoch (system start or event trigger)	No	1	9	Yes
type	Returns the name of the event	6	1	9	Yes

Element Object

The collections, properties, methods, and events in the following tables can be used on all HTML elements.

Element Object Collections

W3C: W3C Standard.

Collection	Description	W3C
attributes[]	Returns an array of the attributes of an element	Yes
childNodes[]	Returns an array of child nodes for an element	Yes

Element Object Properties

Property	Description	W3C
accessKey	Sets or returns an accesskey for an element	Yes
className	Sets or returns the class attribute of an element	Yes
clientHeight	Returns the viewable height of the content on a page (not including borders, margins, or scrollbars)	Yes
clientWidth	Returns the viewable width of the content on a page (not including borders, margins, or scrollbars)	Yes
dir	Sets or returns the text direction of an element	Yes
disabled	Sets or returns the disabled attribute of an element	Yes
firstChild	Returns the first child of an element	Yes
height	Sets or returns the height attribute of an element	Yes
id	Sets or returns the id of an element	Yes
innerHTML	Sets or returns the HTML contents (+text) of an element	Yes
lang	Sets or returns the language code for an element	Yes

Property	Description	W3C
lastChild	Returns the last child of an element	Yes
length	Does not apply to all objects. See specific object type.	Yes
nextSibling	Returns the element immediately following an element	Yes
nodeName	Returns the tagname of an element (in uppercase)	Yes
nodeType	Returns the type of the element	Yes
nodeValue	Returns the value of the element	Yes
offsetHeight	Returns the height of an element, including borders and padding if any, but not margins	No
offsetLeft	Returns the horizontal offset position of the current element relative to its offset container	Yes
offsetParent	Returns the offset container of an element	Yes
offsetTop	Returns the vertical offset position of the current element relative to its offset container	Yes
offsetWidth	Returns the width of an element, including borders and padding if any, but not margins	No
ownerDocument	Returns the root element (document object) for an element	Yes
parentNode	Returns the parent node of an element	Yes
previousSibling	Returns the element immediately before an element	Yes
scrollHeight	Returns the entire height of an element (including areas hidden with scrollbars)	Yes
scrollLeft	Returns the distance between the actual left edge of an element and its left edge currently in view	Yes
scrollTop	Returns the distance between the actual top edge of an element and its top edge currently in view	Yes
scrollWidth	Returns the entire width of an element (including areas hidden with scrollbars)	Yes
style	Sets or returns the style attribute of an element	Yes
tabIndex	Sets or returns the tab order of an element	Yes
tagName	Returns the tagname of an element as a string (in uppercase)	Yes
title	Sets or returns the title attribute of an element	Yes
width	Sets or returns the width attribute of an element	Yes

Element Object Methods

Method	Description	W3C
appendChild()	Adds a new child element to the end of the list of children of the element	Yes
blur()	Removes focus from an element	Yes
click()	Executes a click on an element	Yes
cloneNode()	Clones an element	Yes
focus()	Gives focus to an element	Yes
getAttribute()	Returns the value of an attribute	Yes
getElementsByTagName()	Accesses all elements with a specified tagname	Yes

(continued)

219

(continued)

Method	Description	W3C
hasChildNodes()	Returns whether an element has any child elements	Yes
insertBefore()	Inserts a new child element before an existing child element	Yes
item()	Returns an element based on its index within the document tree	Yes
normalize()	Puts all text nodes underneath this element (including attributes) into a "normal" form where only structure (for example, elements, comments, processing instructions, CDATA sections, and entity references) separates Text nodes, that is, there are neither adjacent Text nodes nor empty Text nodes	Yes
removeAttribute()	Removes a specified attribute from an element	Yes
removeChild()	Removes a child element	Yes
replaceChild()	Replaces a child element	Yes
setAttribute()	Adds a new attribute to an element	Yes
toString()	Converts an element to a string	Yes

Element Object Events

Event	Description	W3C
onblur	When an element loses focus	Yes
onclick	When a mouse clicks on an element	Yes
ondblclick	When a mouse double-clicks on an element	Yes
onfocus	When an element gets focus	Yes
onkeydown	When a keyboard key is pressed	Yes
onkeypress	When a keyboard key is pressed or held down	Yes
onkeyup	When a keyboard key is released	Yes
onmousedown	When a mouse button is pressed	Yes
onmousemove	When the mouse is moved	Yes
onmouseout	When the mouse cursor leaves an element	Yes
onmouseover	When the mouse cursor enters an element	Yes
onmouseup	When a mouse button is released	Yes
onresize	When an element is resized	Yes

Anchor Object

The Anchor object represents an HTML hyperlink.

For each <a> tag in an HTML document, an Anchor object is created.

An anchor allows you to create a link to another document (with the href attribute) or to a different point in the same document (with the name attribute).

You can access an anchor by using getElementById() or by searching through the anchors[] array of the Document object.

Anchor Object Properties

W3C: W3C Standard.

Property	Description	W3C
charset	Sets or returns the value of the charset attribute of a link	Yes
href	Sets or returns the value of the href attribute of a link	Yes
hreflang	Sets or returns the value of the hreflang attribute of a link	Yes
name	Sets or returns the value of the name attribute of a link	Yes
rel	Sets or returns the value of the rel attribute of a link	Yes
rev	Sets or returns the value of the rev attribute of a link	Yes
target	Sets or returns the value of the target attribute of a link	Yes
type	Sets or returns the value of the type attribute of a link	Yes

Standard Properties, Methods, and Events

The Anchor object also supports the standard properties, methods, and events.

Area Object

The Area object represents an area inside an HTML image map (an image map is an image with clickable areas).

For each `<area>` tag in an HTML document, an Area object is created.

Area Object Properties

W3C: W3C Standard.

Property	Description	W3C
alt	Sets or returns the value of the alt attribute of an area	Yes
coords	Sets or returns the value of the coords attribute of an area	Yes
hash	Sets or returns the anchor part of the href attribute value	Yes
host	Sets or returns the hostname:port part of the href attribute value	Yes
hostname	Sets or returns the hostname part of the href attribute value	Yes
href	Sets or returns the value of the href attribute of an area	Yes
noHref	Sets or returns the value of the nohref attribute of an area	Yes
pathname	Sets or returns the pathname part of the href attribute value	Yes
port	Sets or returns the port part of the href attribute value	Yes
protocol	Sets or returns the protocol part of the href attribute value	Yes
search	Sets or returns the querystring part of the href attribute value	Yes
shape	Sets or returns the value of the shape attribute of an area	Yes
target	Sets or returns the value of the target attribute of an area	Yes

Standard Properties, Methods, and Events

The Area object also supports the standard properties, methods, and events.

Base Object

The Base object represents an HTML base element.

The base element is used to specify a default address or a default target for all links on a page.

For each `<base>` tag in an HTML document, a Base object is created.

Base Object Properties

W3C: W3C Standard.

Property	Description	W3C
href	Sets or returns the value of the href attribute in a base element	Yes
target	Sets or returns the value of the target attribute in a base element	Yes

Standard Properties, Methods, and Events

The Base object also supports the standard properties, methods, and events.

Body Object

The Body object represents the HTML body element.

The Body element defines a document's body.

The Body element contains all the contents of an HTML document, such as text, hyperlinks, images, tables, lists, and so on.

Body Object Properties

W3C: W3C Standard.

Property	Description	W3C
aLink	Sets or returns the value of the alink attribute of the body element	Yes
background	Sets or returns the value of the background attribute of the body element	Yes
bgColor	Sets or returns the value of the bgcolor attribute of the body element	Yes
link	Sets or returns the value of the link attribute of the body element	Yes
text	Sets or returns the value of the text attribute of the body element	Yes
vLink	Sets or returns the value of the vlink attribute of the body element	Yes

Standard Properties, Methods, and Events

The Body object also supports the standard properties, methods, and events.

Button Object (Push Button)

The Button object represents a Button Object (Push Button).

For each `<button>` tag in an HTML document, a Button object is created.

Inside an HTML Button element you can put content like text or images. This is the difference between this element and buttons created with the input element.

Button Object Properties

W3C: W3C Standard.

Property	Description	W3C
form	Returns a reference to the form that contains a button	Yes
name	Sets or returns the value of the name attribute of a button	Yes
type	Sets or returns the type of a button	Yes
value	Sets or returns the value of the value attribute of a button	Yes

Standard Properties, Methods, and Events

The Button object also supports the standard properties, methods, and events.

Form Object

The Form object represents an HTML form.

For each `<form>` tag in an HTML document, a Form object is created.

Forms are used to collect user input and contain input elements like text fields, check boxes, radio buttons, Submit buttons, and more. A form also can contain select menus and `textarea`, `fieldset`, `legend`, and `label` elements.

Forms are used to pass data to a server.

Form Object Collections

W3C: W3C Standard.

Collection	Description	W3C
elements[]	Returns an array of all elements in a form	Yes

Form Object Properties

Property	Description	W3C
acceptCharset	Sets or returns the value of the accept-charset attribute in a form	Yes
action	Sets or returns the value of the action attribute in a form	Yes
enctype	Sets or returns the value of the enctype attribute in a form	Yes
length	Returns the number of elements in a form	Yes
method	Sets or returns the value of the method attribute in a form	Yes
name	Sets or returns the value of the name attribute in a form	Yes
target	Sets or returns the value of the target attribute in a form	Yes

Form Object Methods

Method	Description	W3C
reset()	Resets a form	Yes
submit()	Submits a form	Yes

Form Object Events

Event	The event occurs when...	W3C
onreset	The Reset button is clicked	Yes
onsubmit	The Submit button is clicked	Yes

Standard Properties, Methods, and Events

The Form object also supports the standard properties, methods, and events.

Frame/IFrame Object

The Frame object represents an HTML frame.

The <frame> tag defines one particular window (frame) within a frameset.

For each <frame> tag in an HTML document, a Frame object is created.

The IFrame object represents an HTML inline frame.

The <iframe> tag defines an inline frame that contains another document.

For each <iframe> tag in an HTML document, an IFrame object is created.

Frame/IFrame Object Properties

W3C: W3C Standard.

Property	Description	W3C
align	Sets or returns the value of the align attribute in an iframe	Yes
contentDocument	Returns the document object generated by a frame/iframe	Yes
contentWindow	Returns the window object generated by a frame/iframe	No
frameBorder	Sets or returns the value of the frameborder attribute in a frame/iframe	Yes
height	Sets or returns the value of the height attribute in an iframe	Yes
longDesc	Sets or returns the value of the longdesc attribute in a frame/iframe	Yes
marginHeight	Sets or returns the value of the marginheight attribute in a frame/iframe	Yes
marginWidth	Sets or returns the value of the marginwidth attribute in a frame/iframe	Yes
name	Sets or returns the value of the name attribute in a frame/iframe	Yes
noResize	Sets or returns the value of the noresize attribute in a frame	Yes
scrolling	Sets or returns the value of the scrolling attribute in a frame/iframe	Yes
src	Sets or returns the value of the src attribute in a frame/iframe	Yes
width	Sets or returns the value of the width attribute in an iframe	Yes

Standard Properties, Methods, and Events

The Frame and IFrame objects also support the standard properties, methods, and events.

Frameset Object

The Frameset object represents an HTML frameset.

The HTML frameset element holds two or more frame elements. Each frame element holds a separate document.

The HTML frameset element states only how many columns or rows there will be in the frameset.

Frameset Object Properties

W3C: W3C Standard.

Property	Description	W3C
border	Sets or returns the width of the border between frames	Yes
cols	Sets or returns the value of the cols attribute in a frameset	Yes
rows	Sets or returns the value of the rows attribute in a frameset	Yes

Frameset Object Events

Event	Description	W3C
onload	Script to be run when a document loads	Yes

Standard Properties, Methods, and Events

The Frameset object also supports the standard properties, methods, and events.

Image Object

The Image object represents an embedded image.

For each <img> tag in an HTML document, an Image object is created.

Image Object Properties

W3C: W3C Standard.

Property	Description	W3C
align	Sets or returns how to align an image according to the surrounding text	Yes
alt	Sets or returns an alternate text to be displayed if a browser cannot show an image	Yes
border	Sets or returns the border around an image	Yes
complete	Returns whether the browser has finished loading the image	No
height	Sets or returns the height of an image	Yes
href		
hspace	Sets or returns the white space on the left and right side of the image	Yes
isMap	Returns whether an image is a server-side image map	Yes
longDesc	Sets or returns a URL to a document containing a description of the image	Yes
lowsrc	Sets or returns a URL to a low-resolution version of an image	No
name	Sets or returns the name of an image	Yes
src	Sets or returns the URL of an image	Yes
useMap	Sets or returns the value of the usemap attribute of a client-side image map	Yes
vspace	Sets or returns the white space on the top and bottom of the image	Yes
width	Sets or returns the width of an image	Yes

Image Object Events

Event	The event occurs when...	W3C
onabort	Loading of an image is interrupted	Yes
onerror	An error occurs when loading an image	Yes
onload	An image is finished loading	Yes

Standard Properties, Methods, and Events

The Image object also supports the standard properties, methods, and events.

Button Object

The Button object represents a button in an HTML form.

For each instance of an `<input type="button">` tag in an HTML form, a Button object is created.

You can access a button by searching through the `elements[]` array of the form or by using `document.getElementById()`.

Button Object Properties

W3C: W3C Standard.

Property	Description	W3C
alt	Sets or returns an alternate text to display if a browser does not support buttons	Yes
disabled	Sets or returns whether a button should be disabled	Yes
form	Returns a reference to the form that contains the button	Yes
name	Sets or returns the name of a button	Yes
type	Returns the type of form element a button is	Yes
value	Sets or returns the text that is displayed on the button	Yes

Standard Properties, Methods, and Events

The Button object also supports the standard properties, methods, and events.

Checkbox Object

The Checkbox object represents a check box in an HTML form.

For each `<input type="checkbox">` tag in an HTML form, a Checkbox object is created.

You can access a check box by searching through the `elements[]` array of the form, or by using `document.getElementById()`.

227

Checkbox Object Properties

W3C: W3C Standard.

Property	Description	W3C
alt	Sets or returns an alternate text to display if a browser does not support check boxes	Yes
checked	Sets or returns whether a check box should be checked	Yes
defaultChecked	Returns the default value of the checked attribute	Yes
disabled	Sets or returns whether a check box should be disabled	Yes
form	Returns a reference to the form that contains the check box	Yes
name	Sets or returns the name of a check box	Yes
type	Returns the type of form element a check box is	Yes
value	Sets or returns the value of the value attribute of a check box	Yes

Standard Properties, Methods, and Events

The Checkbox object also supports the standard properties, methods, and events.

FileUpload Object

For each `<input type="file">` tag in an HTML form, a FileUpload object is created.

You can access a FileUpload object by searching through the `elements[]` array of the form or by using `document.getElementById()`.

FileUpload Object Properties

W3C: W3C Standard.

Property	Description	W3C
accept	Sets or returns a comma-separated list of MIME types that indicates the MIME type of the file transfer	Yes
alt	Sets or returns an alternate text to display if the browser does not support `<input type="file">`	Yes
defaultValue	Sets or returns the initial value of the FileUpload object	Yes
disabled	Sets or returns whether the FileUpload object should be disabled	Yes
form	Returns a reference to the form that contains the FileUpload object	Yes
name	Sets or returns the name of the FileUpload object	Yes
type	Returns the type of the form element. For a FileUpload object it will be "file"	Yes
value	Returns the filename of the FileUpload object after the text is set by user input	Yes

FileUpload Object Methods

Method	Description	W3C
select()	Selects the FileUpload object	Yes

Standard Properties, Methods, and Events

The FileUpload object also supports the standard properties, methods, and events.

Hidden Object

The Hidden object represents a hidden input field in an HTML form.

For each `<input type="hidden">` tag in an HTML form, a Hidden object is created.

You can access a hidden input field by searching through the `elements[]` array of the form, or by using `document.getElementById()`.

Hidden Object Properties

W3C: W3C Standard.

Property	Description	W3C
alt	Sets or returns an alternate text to display if a browser does not support hidden fields	Yes
form	Returns a reference to the form that contains the hidden field	Yes
name	Sets or returns the name of a hidden field	Yes
type	Returns the type of form element a hidden input field is	Yes
value	Sets or returns the value of the value attribute of the hidden field	Yes

Standard Properties, Methods, and Events

The Hidden object also supports the standard properties, methods, and events.

Password Object

The Password object represents a password field in an HTML form.

For each `<input type="password">` tag in an HTML form, a Password object is created.

You can access a password field by searching through the `elements[]` array of the form or by using `document.getElementById()`.

Password Object Properties

W3C: W3C Standard.

Property	Description	W3C
alt	Sets or returns an alternate text to display if a browser does not support password fields	Yes
defaultValue	Sets or returns the default value of a password field	Yes
disabled	Sets or returns whether a password field should be disabled	Yes
form	Returns a reference to the form that contains the password field	Yes
maxLength	Sets or returns the maximum number of characters in a password field	Yes
name	Sets or returns the name of a password field	Yes
readOnly	Sets or returns whether a password field should be read-only	Yes
size	Sets or returns the size of a password field	Yes
type	Returns the type of form element a password field is	Yes
value	Sets or returns the value of the value attribute of the password field	Yes

Password Object Methods

Method	Description	W3C
select()	Selects the text in a password field	Yes

Standard Properties, Methods, and Events

The Password object also supports the standard properties, methods, and events.

Radio Object

The Radio object represents a radio button in an HTML form.

For each `<input type="radio">` tag in an HTML form, a Radio object is created.

You can access a Radio object by searching through the `elements[]` array of the form or by using `document.getElementById()`.

Radio Object Properties

W3C: W3C Standard.

Property	Description	W3C
alt	Sets or returns an alternate text to display if a browser does not support radio buttons	Yes
checked	Sets or returns the state of a radio button	Yes
defaultChecked	Returns the default state of a radio button	Yes

Property	Description	W3C
disabled	Sets or returns whether a radio button should be disabled	Yes
form	Returns a reference to the form that contains the radio button	Yes
name	Sets or returns the name of a radio button	Yes
type	Returns the type of form element a radio button is	Yes
value	Sets or returns the value of the value attribute of the radio button	Yes

Standard Properties, Methods, and Events

The Radio object also supports the standard properties, methods, and events.

Reset Object

The Reset object represents a reset button in an HTML form.

For each `<input type="reset">` tag in an HTML form, a Reset object is created.

You can access a reset button by searching through the `elements[]` array of the form or by using `document.getElementById()`.

Reset Object Properties

W3C: W3C Standard.

Property	Description	W3C
alt	Sets or returns an alternate text to display if a browser does not support reset buttons	Yes
disabled	Sets or returns whether a reset button should be disabled	Yes
form	Returns a reference to the form that contains the reset button	Yes
name	Sets or returns the name of a reset button	Yes
type	Returns the type of form element a reset button is	Yes
value	Sets or returns the text that is displayed on a reset button	Yes

Standard Properties, Methods, and Events

The Reset object also supports the standard properties, methods, and events.

Submit Object

The Submit object represents a submit button in an HTML form.

For each `<input type="submit">` tag in an HTML form, a Submit object is created.

Example: Form validation

You can access a submit button by searching through the `elements[]` array of the form or by using `document.getElementById()`.

Submit Object Properties

W3C: W3C Standard.

Property	Description	W3C
alt	Sets or returns an alternate text to display if a browser does not support submit buttons	Yes
disabled	Sets or returns whether a submit button should be disabled	Yes
form	Returns a reference to the form that contains the submit button	Yes
name	Sets or returns the name of a submit button	Yes
type	Returns the type of form element a submit button is	Yes
value	Sets or returns the text that is displayed on a submit button	Yes

Standard Properties, Methods, and Events

The Submit object also supports the standard properties, methods, and events.

Text Object

The Text object represents a text-input field in an HTML form.

For each `<input type="text">` tag in an HTML form, a Text object is created.

You can access a text-input field by searching through the `elements[]` array of the form, or by using `document.getElementById()`.

Text Object Properties

W3C: W3C Standard.

Property	Description	W3C
alt	Sets or returns an alternate text to display if a browser does not support text fields	Yes
defaultValue	Sets or returns the default value of a text field	Yes
disabled	Sets or returns whether a text field should be disabled	Yes
form	Returns a reference to the form that contains the text field	Yes
maxLength	Sets or returns the maximum number of characters in a text field	Yes
name	Sets or returns the name of a text field	Yes
readOnly	Sets or returns whether a text field should be read-only	Yes
size	Sets or returns the size of a text field	Yes
type	Returns the type of form element a text field is	Yes
value	Sets or returns the value of the value attribute of a text field	Yes

Text Object Methods

Method	Description	W3C
select()	Selects the content of a text field	Yes

Standard Properties, Methods, and Events

The Text object also supports the standard properties, methods, and events.

Link Object

The Link object represents an HTML link element.

A link element defines the relationship between two linked documents.

The link element is defined in the head section of an HTML document.

Link Object Properties

W3C: W3C Standard.

Property	Description	W3C
charset	Sets or returns the character encoding of the target URL	Yes
disabled	Sets or returns whether the target URL should be disabled	Yes
href	Sets or returns the URL of a linked resource	Yes
hreflang	Sets or returns the base language of the target URL	Yes
media	Sets or returns on what device the document will be displayed	Yes
name	Sets or returns the name of a <link> element	Yes
rel	Sets or returns the relationship between the current document and the target URL	Yes
rev	Sets or returns the relationship between the target URL and the current document	Yes
type	Sets or returns the MIME type of the target URL	Yes

Standard Properties, Methods, and Events

The Link object also supports the standard properties, methods, and events.

Meta Object

The Meta object represents an HTML meta element.

Metadata is information about data.

The <meta> tag provides metadata about the HTML document. Metadata will not be displayed on the page, but will be machine parsable.

Meta elements are typically used to specify page description, keywords, author of the document, last modified, and other metadata.

The `<meta>` tag always goes inside the head element.

Meta Object Properties

W3C: W3C Standard.

Property	Description	W3C
content	Sets or returns the value of the content attribute of a `<meta>` element	Yes
httpEquiv	Connects the content attribute to an HTTP header	Yes
name	Connects the content attribute to a name	Yes
scheme	Sets or returns the format to be used to interpret the value of the content attribute	Yes

Standard Properties, Methods, and Events

The Meta object also supports the standard properties, methods, and events.

Object Object

The Object object represents an HTML object element.

The `<object>` tag is used to include objects such as images, audio, videos, Java applets, ActiveX, PDF, and Flash into a Web page.

Object Object Properties

W3C: W3C Standard.

Property	Description	W3C
align	Sets or returns the alignment of the object according to the surrounding text	Yes
archive	Sets or returns a string that can be used to implement your own archive functionality for the object	Yes
border	Sets or returns the border around the object	Yes
code	Sets or returns the URL of the file that contains the compiled Java class	Yes
codeBase	Sets or returns the URL of the component	Yes
codeType	Sets or retrieves the Internet media type for the code associated with the object. Read only.	Yes
data	A URL specifying the location of the object's data	Yes
declare	Declare (for future reference), but do not instantiate, this object	Yes
form	Returns a reference to the object's parent form	Yes

Property	Description	W3C
height	Sets or returns the height of the object	Yes
hspace	Sets or returns the horizontal margin of the object	Yes
name	Sets or returns the name of the object	Yes
standby	Sets or returns a message when loading the object	Yes
type	Sets or returns the content type for data downloaded via the data attribute	Yes
useMap	Use client-side image map	Yes
vspace	Sets or returns the vertical margin of the object	Yes
width	Sets or returns the width of the object	Yes

Standard Properties, Methods, and Events

The Object object also supports the standard properties, methods, and events.

Option Object

The Option object represents an option in a drop-down list in an HTML form.

For each <option> tag in an HTML form, an Option object is created.

You can access an Option object by searching through the elements[] array of the form, or by using document.getElementById().

Option Object Properties

W3C: W3C Standard.

Property	Description	W3C
defaultSelected	Returns the default value of the selected attribute	Yes
disabled	Sets or returns whether an option should be disabled	Yes
form	Returns a reference to the form that contains an option	Yes
index	Returns the index position of an option in a drop-down list	Yes
label	Sets or returns a label for an option (only for option-groups)	Yes
selected	Sets or returns the value of the selected attribute	Yes
text	Sets or returns the text value of an option	Yes
value	Sets or returns the value to be sent to the server	Yes

Standard Properties, Methods, and Events

The Option object also supports the standard properties, methods, and events.

Select Object

The Select object represents a drop-down list in an HTML form.

For each `<select>` tag in an HTML form, a Select object is created.

You can access a Select object by searching through the `elements[]` array of the form or by using `document.getElementById()`.

Select Object Collections

W3C: W3C Standard.

Collection	Description	W3C
options[]	Returns an array of all the options in a drop-down list	Yes

Select Object Properties

Property	Description	W3C
disabled	Sets or returns whether a drop-down list should be disabled	Yes
form	Returns a reference to the form that contains the drop-down list	Yes
length	Returns the number of options in a drop-down list	Yes
multiple	Sets or returns whether multiple items can be selected	Yes
name	Sets or returns the name of a drop-down list	Yes
selectedIndex	Sets or returns the index of the selected option in a drop-down list	Yes
size	Sets or returns the number of visible rows in a drop-down list	Yes
type	Returns the type of form element a drop-down list is	Yes

Select Object Methods

Method	Description	W3C
add()	Adds an option to a drop-down list	Yes
remove()	Removes an option from a drop-down list	Yes

Standard Properties, Methods, and Events

The Select object also supports the standard properties, methods, and events.

Style Object

The Style object represents an individual style statement.

The Style object can be accessed from the document or from the elements to which that style is applied.

Syntax for using the Style object properties:

```
document.getElementById("id").style.property="value"
```

The Style object property categories are as follows:

- ▶▶ Background
- ▶▶ Border and Margin
- ▶▶ Layout
- ▶▶ List
- ▶▶ Misc
- ▶▶ Positioning
- ▶▶ Printing
- ▶▶ Table
- ▶▶ Text

Background Properties

W3C: W3C Standard.

Property	Description	W3C
background	Sets all background properties	Yes
backgroundAttachment	Sets whether a background-image is fixed or scrolls with the page	Yes
backgroundColor	Sets the background-color of an element	Yes
backgroundImage	Sets the background-image of an element	Yes
backgroundPosition	Sets the starting position of a background-image	Yes
backgroundPositionX	Sets the x-coordinates of the backgroundPosition property	No
backgroundPositionY	Sets the y-coordinates of the backgroundPosition property	No
backgroundRepeat	Sets if/how a background-image will be repeated	Yes

Border and Margin Properties

Property	Description	W3C
border	Sets all properties for the four borders	Yes
borderBottom	Sets all properties for the bottom border	Yes
borderBottomColor	Sets the color of the bottom border	Yes
borderBottomStyle	Sets the style of the bottom border	Yes
borderBottomWidth	Sets the width of the bottom border	Yes

(continued)

237

(continued)

Property	Description	W3C
borderColor	Sets the color of all four borders (can have up to four colors)	Yes
borderLeft	Sets all properties for the left border	Yes
borderLeftColor	Sets the color of the left border	Yes
borderLeftStyle	Sets the style of the left border	Yes
borderLeftWidth	Sets the width of the left border	Yes
borderRight	Sets all properties for the right border	Yes
borderRightColor	Sets the color of the right border	Yes
borderRightStyle	Sets the style of the right border	Yes
borderRightWidth	Sets the width of the right border	Yes
borderStyle	Sets the style of all four borders (can have up to four styles)	Yes
borderTop	Sets all properties for the top border	Yes
borderTopColor	Sets the color of the top border	Yes
borderTopStyle	Sets the style of the top border	Yes
borderTopWidth	Sets the width of the top border	Yes
borderWidth	Sets the width of all four borders (can have up to four widths)	Yes
margin	Sets the margins of an element (can have up to four values)	Yes
marginBottom	Sets the bottom margin of an element	Yes
marginLeft	Sets the left margin of an element	Yes
marginRight	Sets the right margin of an element	Yes
marginTop	Sets the top margin of an element	Yes
outline	Sets all outline properties	Yes
outlineColor	Sets the color of the outline around a element	Yes
outlineStyle	Sets the style of the outline around an element	Yes
outlineWidth	Sets the width of the outline around an element	Yes
padding	Sets the padding of an element (can have up to four values)	Yes
paddingBottom	Sets the bottom padding of an element	Yes
paddingLeft	Sets the left padding of an element	Yes
paddingRight	Sets the right padding of an element	Yes
paddingTop	Sets the top padding of an element	Yes

Layout Properties

Property	Description	W3C
clear	Sets on which sides of an element other floating elements are not allowed	Yes
clip	Sets the shape of an element	Yes
content	Sets meta-information	Yes
counterIncrement	Sets a list of counter names, followed by an integer. The integer indicates by how much the counter is incremented for every occurrence of the element. The default is 1	Yes
counterReset	Sets a list of counter names, followed by an integer. The integer gives the value that the counter is set to on each occurrence of the element. The default is 0	Yes

Property	Description	W3C
cssFloat	Sets where an image or a text will appear (float) in another element	Yes
cursor	Sets the type of cursor to be displayed	Yes
direction	Sets the text direction of an element	Yes
display	Sets how an element will be displayed	Yes
height	Sets the height of an element	Yes
markerOffset	Sets the distance between the nearest border edges of a marker box and its principal box	Yes
marks	Sets whether cross marks or crop marks should be rendered just outside the page box edge	Yes
maxHeight	Sets the maximum height of an element	Yes
maxWidth	Sets the maximum width of an element	Yes
minHeight	Sets the minimum height of an element	Yes
minWidth	Sets the minimum width of an element	Yes
overflow	Specifies what to do with content that does not fit in an element box	Yes
verticalAlign	Sets the vertical alignment of content in an element	Yes
visibility	Sets whether an element should be visible	Yes
width	Sets the width of an element	Yes

List Properties

Property	Description	W3C
listStyle	Sets all the properties for a list	Yes
listStyleImage	Sets an image as the list-item marker	Yes
listStylePosition	Positions the list-item marker	Yes
listStyleType	Sets the list-item marker type	Yes

Misc Properties

Property	Description	W3C
cssText	Contains the entire contents of the stylesheet. **IE only property**	

Positioning Properties

Property	Description	W3C
bottom	Sets how far the bottom edge of an element is above/below the bottom edge of the parent element	Yes
left	Sets how far the left edge of an element is to the right/left of the left edge of the parent element	Yes
position	Places an element in a static, relative, absolute, or fixed position	Yes

(continued)

239

(continued)

Property	Description	W3C
right	Sets how far the right edge of an element is to the left/right of the right edge of the parent element	Yes
top	Sets how far the top edge of an element is above/below the top edge of the parent element	Yes
zIndex	Sets the stack order of an element	Yes

Printing Properties

Property	Description	W3C
orphans	Sets the minimum number of lines for a paragraph that must be left at the bottom of a page	Yes
page	Sets a page type to use when displaying an element	Yes
pageBreakAfter	Sets the page-breaking behavior after an element	Yes
pageBreakBefore	Sets the page-breaking behavior before an element	Yes
pageBreakInside	Sets the page-breaking behavior inside an element	Yes
size	Sets the orientation and size of a page	Yes
widows	Sets the minimum number of lines for a paragraph that must be left at the top of a page	Yes

Table Properties

Property	Description	W3C
borderCollapse	Sets whether the table borders are collapsed into a single border or detached as in standard HTML	Yes
borderSpacing	Sets the distance that separates cell borders	Yes
captionSide	Sets the position of the table caption	Yes
emptyCells	Sets whether to show empty cells in a table	Yes
tableLayout	Sets the algorithm used to display the table cells, rows, and columns	Yes

Text Properties

Property	Description	W3C
color	Sets the color of the text	Yes
font	Sets all font properties	Yes
fontFamily	Sets the font of an element	Yes
fontSize	Sets the font-size of an element	Yes
fontSizeAdjust	Sets/adjusts the size of text	Yes
fontStretch	Sets how to condense or stretch a font	Yes
fontStyle	Sets the font-style of an element	Yes
fontVariant	Displays text in a small-caps font	Yes
fontWeight	Sets the boldness of the font	Yes
letterSpacing	Sets the space between characters	Yes
lineHeight	Sets the distance between lines	Yes

Property	Description	W3C
quotes	Sets which quotation marks to use in text	Yes
textAlign	Aligns the text	Yes
textDecoration	Sets the decoration of text	Yes
textIndent	Indents the first line of text	Yes
textShadow	Sets the shadow effect of text	Yes
textTransform	Sets capitalization effect on text	Yes
unicodeBidi	Sets the Unicode bidirectional property	Yes
whiteSpace	Sets how to handle line breaks and white space in text	Yes
wordSpacing	Sets the space between words in a text	Yes

Table Object

The Table object represents an HTML table.

For each `<table>` tag in an HTML document, a Table object is created.

Table Object Collections

W3C: W3C Standard.

Collection	Description	W3C
cells[]	Returns an array containing each cell in a table	No
rows[]	Returns an array containing each row in a table	Yes
tBodies[]	Returns an array containing each tbody in a table	Yes

Table Object Properties

Property	Description	W3C
border	Sets or returns the width of the table border	Yes
caption	Sets or returns the caption of a table	Yes
cellPadding	Sets or returns the amount of space between the cell border and cell content	Yes
cellSpacing	Sets or returns the amount of space between the cells in a table	Yes
frame	Sets or returns the outer borders of a table	Yes
rules	Sets or returns the inner borders of a table	Yes
summary	Sets or returns a description of a table	Yes
tFoot	Returns the tFoot object of a table	Yes
tHead	Returns the tHead object of a table	Yes
width	Sets or returns the width of a table	Yes

Table Object Methods

Method	Description	W3C
createCaption()	Creates a caption element for a table	Yes
createTFoot()	Creates an empty tFoot element in a table	Yes
createTHead()	Creates an empty tHead element in a table	Yes
deleteCaption()	Deletes the caption element and its content from a table	Yes
deleteRow()	Deletes a row from a table	Yes
deleteTFoot()	Deletes the tFoot element and its content from a table	Yes
deleteTHead()	Deletes the tHead element and its content from a table	Yes
insertRow()	Inserts a new row in a table	Yes

Standard Properties, Methods, and Events

The Table object also supports the standard properties, methods, and events.

TableCell Object

The TableCell object represents an HTML table cell.

For each <td> tag in an HTML document, a TableCell object is created.

TableCell Object Properties

W3C: W3C Standard.

Property	Description	W3C
abbr	Sets or returns an abbreviated version of the content in a table cell	Yes
align	Sets or returns the horizontal alignment of data within a table cell	Yes
axis	Sets or returns a comma-delimited list of related table cells	Yes
cellIndex	Returns the position of a cell in the cells collection of a row	Yes
ch	Sets or returns the alignment character for a table cell	Yes
chOff	Sets or returns the offset of alignment character for a table cell	Yes
colSpan	Sets or returns the number of columns a table cell should span	Yes
headers	Sets or returns a list of space-separated header-cell ids	Yes
rowSpan	Sets or returns the number of rows a table cell should span	Yes
scope	Sets or returns if this cell provides header information	Yes
vAlign	Sets or returns the vertical alignment of data within a table cell	Yes
width	Sets or returns the width of a table cell	Yes

Standard Properties, Methods, and Events

The TableCell object also supports the standard properties, methods, and events.

TableRow Object

The TableRow object represents an HTML table row.

For each <tr> tag in an HTML document, a TableRow object is created.

TableRow Object Collections

W3C: W3C Standard.

Collection	Description	W3C
cells[]	Returns an array containing each cell in the table row	Yes

TableRow Object Properties

Property	Description	W3C
align	Sets or returns the horizontal alignment of data within a table row	Yes
ch	Sets or returns the alignment character for cells in a table row	Yes
chOff	Sets or returns the offset of alignment character for the cells in a table row	Yes
rowIndex	Returns the position of a row in the table's rows collection	Yes
sectionRowIndex	Returns the position of a row in the tBody, tHead, or tFoot rows collection	Yes
vAlign	Sets or returns the vertical alignment of data within a table row	Yes

TableRow Object Methods

Method	Description	W3C
deleteCell()	Deletes a cell in a table row	Yes
insertCell()	Inserts a cell in a table row	Yes

Standard Properties, Methods, and Events

The TableRow object also supports the standard properties, methods, and events.

Textarea Object

The Textarea object represents a text-area in an HTML form.

For each <textarea> tag in an HTML form, a Textarea object is created.

You can access a Textarea object by indexing the elements array (by number or name) of the form or by using getElementById().

Textarea Object Properties

W3C: W3C Standard.

Property	Description	W3C
cols	Sets or returns the width of a textarea	Yes
defaultValue	Sets or returns the default text in a textarea	Yes
disabled	Sets or returns whether a textarea should be disabled	Yes
form	Returns a reference to the form that contains the textarea	Yes
name	Sets or returns the name of a textarea	Yes
readOnly	Sets or returns whether a textarea should be read-only	Yes
rows	Sets or returns the height of a textarea	Yes
Property	Description	W3C
type	Returns the type of the form element	Yes
value	Sets or returns the text in a textarea	Yes

Textarea Object Methods

Method	Description	W3C
select()	Selects the text in a textarea	Yes

Standard Properties, Methods, and Events

The Textarea object also supports the standard properties, methods, and events.

Index